GHOST STORIES
of the SEA

by Barbara Smith

GHOST
HOUSE

Ghost House Books

© 2003 by Ghost House Books and Barbara Smith
First printed in 2003 10 9 8 7 6 5 4 3 2 1
Printed in Canada

The Publisher: Ghost House Books
Distributed by Lone Pine Publishing
10145 – 81 Avenue
Edmonton, AB, Canada
T6E 1W9
Website: http://www.ghostbooks.net

1808 – B Street NW, Suite 140
Auburn, WA, USA
98001

National Library of Canada Cataloguing in Publication Data
Smith, Barbara, 1947–

Ghost stories of the sea / Barbara Smith.

ISBN 1-894877-23-3

1. Ghost stories. 2. Sea stories. I. Title.
BF1486.S64 2003   133.1'22   C2003-910736-1

Editorial Director: Nancy Foulds
Project Editor: Shelagh Kubish
Illustrations Coordinator: Carol Woo
Production Manager: Gene Longson
Cover Design: Gerry Dotto
Layout & Production: Lynett McKell, Ian Dawe, Arlana Anderson-Hale

Photo Credits: Every effort has been made to accurately credit photographers. Any errors or omissions should be directed to the publisher for changes in future editions. Glenbow Archives, Calgary, Canada (p. 47: ND-1-459; p. 145: NA-1338-91; p. 220: NA-1052-7); Barbara Smith (p. 50, 63, 86, 172, 197, 201); National Archives, Still Pictures Branch (p. 90: NWDNS-79-OC-20); FreeFoto/Ian Britton (p. 101); Library of Congress (p. 8, 30: USZ62-71128; p. 33: USZ62-97819; p. 55: PPMSC-00564; p. 61: USZ62-56585; p. 68, 194: USZ62-126591; p. 73, 76: USZ62-76929; p. 78: USZ-89964; p. 83, 94: HABS, VA:,28-HAMP,2J-2; p. 104: HABS, MINN,69-DULU,4-2; p. 116: LC-D4-14258; p. 125: HABS, ME,16-BOONI,1-3; p. 127, 130: HABS, CAL,38-SANFRA,85-1; p. 148, 163: USZ62-90099; p. 175: PPMSC-00554; p. 177: PPMSC-00565).

We acknowledge the financial support of the Government of Canada through the Book Publishing Industry Development Program (BPIDP) for our publishing activities.

PC: P6

In recognition of my husband's
and my father's services
in the Royal Canadian Navy

In the end, the sea will win. It always does.

Contents

Chapter Four: Derelicts

Chapter Five: Strange and Spooky Sea Stories

Chapter Six: Mysterious Areas

Chapter Seven: Phantom Ships

Acknowledgments

No author is solely responsible for the completion of his or her book. In my case, that is especially so. I depend heavily on the talents and generosity of others. Without the Ghost House Books' team behind me, you would not be reading this book. Warm and humble thanks to every one of those talented people. Your contribution to the success of this series is gigantic and, please know, very deeply appreciated. It's an honor to work with all of you. I owe a special debt of gratitude to Grant Kennedy, Shane Kennedy, Nancy Foulds, Shelagh Kubish, Carol Woo and Jeff Fedorkiw.

Researcher W. Ritchie Benedict of Calgary has skillfully and kindly supported my work for many years now. Thank you for your amazing generosity, Ritchie. Dr. Wayne McVey once again took time away from his vacation to take a photograph for me, as has his friendship. Thank you, Wayne. I definitely owe you a cup of coffee! Dr. Barrie Robinson's skills as a precise but gentle first-run editor have become invaluable to me, as has his friendship. Fred Rogers of Qualicum Beach, a man I have never even spoken to, kindly sent me his entire accumulation of research material regarding sea-related ghost stories. How lucky can an author get?

And, as always, I need to publicly thank those closest to me, who support me in all areas of my life—my husband, Bob, my daughters, Debbie and Robyn, and my dear friend Jo-Anne Christensen.

Introduction

Ghosts and the sea are each mysterious. Combined, they are nearly irresistible for those of us who love to explore the unknown.

Sailors are a tight-knit lot and tend to be a superstitious, which really isn't much of a surprise considering that their lives depend on one of nature's most unpredictable and enormous elements—the sea. It is generally accepted in the seafaring community, for example, that renaming a ship will bring bad luck, that no voyage should ever be started on a Friday, and that seeing a phantom ship is a portent of ill.

Perhaps the multitude of ghostly sea stories grew from those, and other, unusual beliefs within the seafaring community. Or did they? After reading the following collection of ghost stories of the sea, you might find reason to believe that the multitude of seafaring superstitions have grown not from sailors' imaginations but from the haunted seas themselves.

1
Ghosts on Board

One of the many superstitions sailors have is that a ghost aboard a ship is absolutely the worst sign of impending bad luck. The following stories certainly illustrate why such a belief has come to be.

Ghosts Galore

When is a haunted ship not a haunted ship? When that haunted ship is the very haunted *Queen Mary*, now a luxurious Long Beach, California, hotel. Fortunately, her current owners appreciate the *Queen Mary*'s paranormal characteristics, because to deny them would be exceedingly naïve. From the very beginning, the *Queen Mary* was destined to have a tremendous impact, not just within shipping circles, but on the world in general—and even beyond.

Launching any ship is an important event. Launching the *Queen Mary* was exceptionally so, especially for her owners, England's Cunard Line, who had invested heavily in this ship's success. She was nearly 1020 feet long and weighed 81,237 gross tons. To put these measurements in a more familiar perspective, the enormous *Titanic* was just over 882 feet and 46,329 gross tons.

As the new pride of their fleet slipped into the water on September 26, 1934, the owners were distressed to hear the proclamation of the well-known Lady Mabel Fortescue-Harrison: "Most of this generation will be gone, including myself, when this event occurs. However, RMS *Queen Mary* will know [her] greatest fame and popularity when she never sails another mile and never carries another passenger."

As she predicted, Fortescue-Harrison did not live to know that her words had been absolutely correct. The British ship that was at one time referred to as the "Queen of the Atlantic" has become a famous and enormously popular floating hotel. According to Elizabeth Borsting, who served as the public relations manager for the *Queen Mary* Hotel in the late 1990s, thousands of yearly guests are "fascinated with the spirits aboard the haunted *Queen Mary*."

And, the ship-turned-hotel has more than earned its haunted status. At least 20 ghosts are still on board—all presumed to be spirits left over from the *Queen Mary*'s sailing days.

During its first six years of operation, the opulent sea liner was popular with royalty, movie stars and business tycoons. Then, four days into the cruise that began on August 30, 1939, with $44 million in gold bullion and 2550 wealthy passengers aboard, the crew was suddenly ordered to cover all the ship's 2000 plus portholes. The lives of all on board suddenly depended on the ship remaining undetected. England and France had just declared war on Germany; the icy waters of the Atlantic were now filled with Nazi warships, U-boats in particular; the skies above were crowded with bombers from Hitler's *Luftwaffe*.

The *Queen Mary* remained undetected throughout the remainder of her voyage. This initial reaction to wartime also served to foreshadow the enormous ship's next incarnation as a troop carrier nicknamed the "*Gray Ghost*." As soon as the *Queen Mary* made port on that last pleasure voyage, she was stripped of her luxurious appointments, and her exterior was painted a dull gray in an apparently successful attempt to continue to hide her from the enemy.

Because it was so dangerous to cross the Atlantic in wartime, the ship's tremendous speed of 28.5 knots was an important attribute. Unfortunately, that speed was also directly responsible for a tragic wartime accident—

and was one of the reasons the ship became haunted. The *Queen Mary* and her much smaller escort, the *Curacoa*, were sailing together. To make their courses difficult for German submarines to track, both surface crafts maintained zigzag patterns. Somehow, a navigational error was made and the huge *Gray Ghost* sailed directly into the *Curacoa*, slicing the escort ship in two.

Of the 439 sailors aboard the escort vessel, 338 perished—many by drowning in the freezing water—as they watched the larger ship sail away in compliance with strict orders not to stop and rescue those in peril. The trauma of both the accident and the orders to sail away and leave the men to drown was so great that it permanently scarred the large ship's psychic atmosphere.

As soon as the *Queen Mary* reached safety, she was repaired with the application of a 70-ton patch of cement. That repair did nothing for the psychic scars the accident had caused. Despite this scarring, the ship continued to serve as an extremely important component in the war effort. Even during the height of the war, England's Prime Minister, Winston Churchill, chose to sail on the *Queen Mary* everytime he had to cross the Atlantic Ocean.

When peace was finally declared in 1945, the luxury-liner-turned-troop-carrier continued to serve soldiers, sailors and airmen, but in a more genteel manner—by making six "bride and baby" crossings, carrying nearly 13,000 war brides and their infants to the United States and Canada. Then for the next 20 years, the *Queen Mary* again traversed the oceans of the world as a passenger liner, occasionally even carrying royalty again.

By December 1967, the *Queen Mary*'s days of active service were over. After 1001 Atlantic crossings, she was purchased by the American city of Long Beach for $3.45 million and permanently docked in Long Beach. Her docking was the first step in the fulfillment of Lady Mabel Fortescue-Harrison's prediction of 31 years earlier. From that day forward, the ship that had already served so many different purposes never carried another passenger, never sailed another mile. Her ship's register was handed over to the British Consul General and she was removed from the British Registry of Ships. Now officially classified as a building, the *Queen Mary*, stationary and dependent on shore-side utilities, has realized her greatest fame and popularity as a tourist attraction, with new hotel, banquet and museum facilities incorporated within the framework of her hull.

Shortly after the ship's arrival at her permanent pier, the owners became all too aware that the vessel's varied past had left it crowded with spirits. One of the most evident hauntings can be found in the section of the hull that hit the *Curacoa*. Ship's staff reported that "a television crew left their audio recorder running overnight in the exact location where the two ships collided. As the tape played back the next day, incredible sounds of pounding could be heard. Others have claimed to hear voices and bloodcurdling noises coming from the same area."

Many people have reported hearing these ghostly sounds. Some describe the pounding in the area as a "frantic knocking" or "strange tapping." Others say that they have heard water gushing and metal tearing—the sounds of that fatal accident replaying on a continuous psychic audio loop into eternity. Even more distressing are the phantom shrieks and moans emanating from that area of the ship. The anguished spirits of the sailors who were either killed on impact or left to drown after the two ships collided have become an atmospheric part of the *Queen Mary* herself.

John Smith, who was the *Queen Mary*'s chief engineer when she was retired from service, reported hearing not only tapping but also the sounds of water rushing into the area that had been damaged by the fatal crash. Smith knew the vessel well, and he made an extensive search to locate the source of the noises. Despite his efforts, he could find no reasonable explanation for the sounds and concluded that he was hearing ghostly echoes from that horrible tragedy of so many years before.

In addition to the psychic damage wrought by the wartime deaths (and a fatal accident during the *Queen Mary*'s original construction), there have, according to current staff, been 48 "untimely deaths" on board the ship. These staff members add that many of those spirits have clearly "stayed with the ship."

John Pedder's ghost is one of those spirits. Doorway 13, well below deck, proved to hold the ultimate in bad luck for the young crewman. On July 10, 1966, the 18-year-old was participating in a routine drill. Something went terribly wrong, and Pedder was crushed to death instantly by the water-tight door closing. Former public relations manager Elizabeth Borsting acknowledged that Pedder's manifestation—a bearded young man clad in blue overalls—is frequently seen "walking the length of Shaft Alley...in the depths of the Engine Room."

These reports come from current crew members as well as visitors to the *Queen Mary*. Nancy Wozny, a former tour guide and security officer with the *Queen Mary*, reported that she felt someone beside her as she was locking up the tour areas one night. "I turned around and saw a man standing behind me," she explained. Although she knew it was always theoretically possible that a visitor could become separated from a tour and be left behind, Nancy doubted that this was the case. The image—with its dirty blue overalls, "beautiful beard," "grossly white" skin and complete lack of facial expression—felt all wrong for a tourist. If Nancy initially suspected she was seeing a ghost, her suspicions were confirmed when the young man's image vanished before her eyes.

The ship's indoor swimming pools still exist, but only for display purposes. They are no longer used by flesh-and-blood swimmers, but two female ghosts continue to take advantage of the first-class aquatic facilities. One tour guide had an especially disturbing sighting. She was aware that she was seeing into "another dimension" because, although the manifestation she observed had form enough to reveal that she was wearing a bathing suit, the vision was "in black and white." Seconds later, the supernatural swimmer disappeared as mysteriously as she had appeared.

Another guide reported seeing a woman wearing a vintage 1930s swimsuit preparing to dive into an almost-dry swimming pool. The guide yelled to the woman to stop, then turned around to call security. As she turned back to focus her attention on the apparently insane or suicidal woman, the guide discovered that the apparition had disappeared.

In 1983, *Queen Mary* employee Lester Hart was on one side of the swimming pool when he saw the image of a blonde woman wearing a long-sleeved white gown, on the opposite deck. The apparition, which he described as being a "hazy image" (and therefore one he was sure was not a living person), locked onto Hart's gaze.

Hart was understandably shaken by the encounter, but at least it provided a bit of preparation for his next experience. One day, while he was working in a shop near the pool, Hart heard water splashing, as though someone were swimming. Because a small amount of water is kept in the pool to prevent deterioration, he suspected that a guest had wandered off-limits to indulge in an unauthorized dip. Dropping what he had been doing, Hart hurried to the pool. It was deserted—but the water near the pool's ladder was moving, and there were wet footprints leading across the deck toward a doorway.

This evidence seemed to indicate that Hart's initial suspicions about the errant guest had been correct, so he followed the path of footprints, assuming that they would lead him to the swimmer. His plan was sound, but unfortunately the wet marks simply stopped as though the feet making them had suddenly vanished. More puzzling still was the fact that the area's highly sensitive alarm system was on but had not been triggered by any motion in the vicinity of the pool.

Hart now knew that he had experienced an encounter with one of the swimming pool ghosts, presumably the one who's been seen wearing the 1930s-style swimsuit. Another spirit is known to haunt that area, but it is usually dressed in street clothes that witnesses have no trouble identifying as being from the 1960s.

At least one more ghost makes a home in the pool area. This one usually manifests itself only as the sound of childish laughter, but oddly the image of a forlorn little boy has occasionally been seen. The lad might not be so sad if he knew that he could find other ghostly playmates on board. In an area of the ship that was once the playroom but is now used for storage, many people have heard the sounds of phantom children playing. An infant who died just hours after being born can also still be heard.

The most imposing ghost aboard the luxurious ship-and-hotel is that of Winston Churchill. Although his spirit is not a constant presence, psychic remnants of smoke from his famous cigars still linger in the stateroom that was once his. The distinctive smoke can sometimes be seen and smelled quite clearly; the phantom traces are very localized and cannot be attributed to the smoking habits of anyone on board at the time—well, not anyone still living, that is.

Churchill's former room is not the only haunted cabin. The ghost of a purser who was murdered during an attempted robbery has rendered Room B-340 too haunted to be rented out. The administration assumes that few hotel guests would willingly endure dodging objects flying around the room, listening to drawers rattling, trying to sleep while their bed is shaking or being grabbed by unseen hands.

There have also been reports of ghostly activity in several other first-class staterooms. According to the ship's administration, "there have been reports of water running in the middle of the night, phones ringing at early hours of the morning and lights suddenly turning on in the middle of the night. Passengers have reported hearing heavy breathing and feeling people tugging at their covers, only to realize that there was no one [alive] in the room with them."

The ghost in the ship's kitchen area is the disembodied spirit of a murdered man. Not surprisingly, it is an extremely angry and restless soul. This haunting dates back to an event during the ship's wartime service as the "*Gray Ghost*," when an enlisted man reportedly attacked a cook. The skirmish quickly became ugly and the victim was thrown into a hot stove. The wronged man's soul still flings dishes around the kitchen and cries out against the injustice brought upon him. He also causes the lights to go on and off when no one can be seen near any light switch, and he will periodically make off with a commonly used kitchen utensil, only to return it later when no one's looking for it.

Not all of the *Queen Mary*'s ghosts are former humans. The barking of a dog, thought to be the ghost of an Irish Setter, still resonates through one area of the ship while the animal eternally frets about his owner. Pets were allowed on the ship when the *Queen Mary* was a luxury liner but, unless you could afford VIP status, any animal you were traveling with had to be kept in one of the kennels on the sundeck. An Englishman who sailed frequently always brought his beloved Irish Setter with him. The dog was well-trained and enjoyed his walks around the ship with his owner, but he also knew that after those outings, he would once again be locked into his kennel.

Because this routine had long been established, the crew was quite surprised one day when the dog, apparently unprovoked, began to howl and to paw at his kennel door as though trying to escape. The person in charge of the area checked on the animal. The dog appeared to be all right physically but was frantically circling around the kennel area, obviously extremely agitated about something.

The kennel supervisor sent a messenger to the owner's cabin, thinking that perhaps the master could settle his pet down. Sadly, this was not to be the case—the man lay dead in his bed. The dog's strange behavior was seemingly a reaction to somehow sensing the death of his beloved friend and owner.

The poor animal was so inconsolable that his mournful howling can still be heard. Many people have tried to follow those sounds to their source, but no matter how close they think they're getting, the ghostly baying still seems to be coming from far away. Perhaps that strange phenomenon can be explained by the fact that the sorrowful animal is now in the great beyond.

The ghost of Senior Second Officer William Stark is easier to pin down because his image is actually seen wandering about the enormous ship. The man died on board the *Queen Mary* in September 1949. While drunk, he mistakenly consumed a bottle of tetrachloride and died almost immediately. Perhaps because he had no idea that his last cocktail was a lethal one, Stark's confused but harmless soul has remained on board the ship.

Another ghostly sailor, wearing his white dress uniform and proudly displaying his ribbons, has also been seen. When he is spotted, witnesses report that the image is distinct but completely transparent.

The phantom that haunts the room that was originally the Main Lounge and is now known as the Queen's Salon is, according to present-day staff, "a beautiful woman clad in a simple white evening gown. Her image is often seen dancing alone in the shadows." During a tour on the ship, one unsuspecting girl described the woman in detail. Still, the guide saw nothing and continued with the tour. The child repeated her observation, not knowing that she was just one in the long list of visitors who had seen this mysterious woman.

An area of the *Queen Mary* called the Pig 'n' Whistle has been decorated to resemble an old English pub. Whatever spirit haunts this room is not always present— but when it is, *everyone* is aware of it. Plates fly off the wall one after another; pictures, and even a clock on the wall, have been found hanging upside down.

People have also glimpsed a specter in white overalls that is apparently still working in areas that were once engine rooms. It is presumed that he is a revenant from the ship's earliest days. Another entity who also seems to know his way around the area below the main deck is invisible but manages to make the chains at the side of a passageway sway as though someone had run along the corridor touching the chain along the way.

The ghost of a well-dressed man haunts an area near the first-class suites. He has dark hair and is wearing a suit that witnesses judge to be from the 1930s. A photographer might have inadvertently snapped the ghost's picture. According to hotel administration, "a tour guide was taking interior photographs. One picture, which captured the cabin's beautiful tinted mirror, was taken from across the room. When the photos were developed, that particular print featured the reflection of a tall, dark-haired man in the mirror. This would not be considered unusual except for the fact that the man in the photo was wearing a 1930s-style suit and did not resemble the tour guide in the least." In closing, the writer noted that, at the time the strange picture was taken, "the tour guide was alone" and certainly was not wearing vintage clothing.

No one knows which of the many ghosts on the *Queen Mary* is responsible for turning lights on and off, for unlocking locked doors and, in some cases, even propping those doors open. It could be the specter who turned skeptical reporter Tom Hennessy into a believer.

In March 1983, Hennessy spent a night alone aboard the ship—a night he'll never forget. By prior agreement, the scribe was left in some of the most haunted areas of the *Queen Mary* for prearranged lengths of time. He was "serving his time"—all 35 minutes of it—in Shaft Alley when something supernatural joined him. Just as he was settling in at the undeniably unappealing spot, he began to hear the ghostly banging that he had been told so much about. Hennessy bravely made his way toward the noise, but just as he came near it, the banging stopped. He turned around to go back to where he'd been; unfortunately, although he had been locked in and was, he thought, completely alone in the engine area, his path was now blocked by a large oil drum. He turned around and went the other way, but he knew he'd eventually have to get back to his original perch, so he tried again. This time, his way was blocked by not one, but two oil drums. Worse, he could feel the catwalk beneath his feet shaking as though someone was walking toward him. Understandably, Hennessy hurried away from the approaching rumble.

Not long after Hennessy had calmed himself from his encounter with the unknown, he had an even more disturbing experience when he suddenly realized he was overhearing a conversation from somewhere in his vicinity. The conversation he heard was distinct enough that he was certain there were three men talking. The trio of voices soon reduced itself to only one, but that single psychic echo was so distinct that Hennessy was able to make out the words "I'm turning the lights off." Fortunately, the terrified reporter was let out of Shaft Alley before being thrust into darkness.

Tom Hennessy left the *Queen Mary* a changed man. There are no reports of him ever again attempting to stay alone in the place. That's not to say that he hasn't been back. Thousands of people visit the haunted *Queen Mary* every year; many come hoping to see at least one of the ghosts—and many do.

And so, in the end, Lady Mabel Fortescue-Harrison, who died in Hollywood in the mid-1950s, was absolutely correct. The *Queen Mary* definitely gained "its greatest fame and popularity" after the grand vessel was docked permanently. Lady Mabel's prediction must have seemed bizarre at the time she made it, but her prophetic words, uttered the day the giant ship was launched, served to permanently connect her to the amazing ship and to seal her place in history.

Strange and Dreadful

People often wonder if the current interest in ghost stories is a recent phenomenon. Through researching material for this and other true ghost story books, I have come to the conclusion that fascination with the paranormal world has a very long history. The accounts reported in this book reflect that truism.

The following is the oldest ghost tale from the sea that I've come across. It was written for publication in London, England, on March 30—in the year 1672!

It seems that "a strange and dreadful apparition" was discovered aboard the ship *Hopewell of London* as she was bound for Newcastle. Captain John Pye led her crew of nine, and all those men swore to the veracity of the incidents reported. The following is Pye's description, much of it in his words and style, of his encounter with a ghost on board the *Hopewell of London*.

"February 22nd, 1671, we sailed from Gravesend… About nine or ten of the clock in the night following…I went to bed. About twelve of the clock in the night I was awaked by a great noise, but saw nothing. I gave it over as a dream."

Captain Pye continued by describing the events of the following night. Less than an hour after going to his bunk and falling asleep, he was awakened by the sound of members of his crew settling into their own beds. He looked around and "saw the perfect face and proportion of a man in a black hat, coat and striped neckcloth." Realizing how impossible this vision was, for it did not resemble any living person on board, Pye began to pray for protection, and the image vanished as mysteriously as it had appeared.

The next few days and nights of the voyage were uneventful, but then the *Hopewell of London* became completely becalmed. This highly unusual situation greatly concerned the ship's master—especially after having seen that image in his cabin. Pye decided that his men were not safe on the ship under these circumstances, and he ordered them to unlash the rowboat from the deck, lower it over the side, board it and row away from the larger craft as quickly as they were able to. Being a true and loyal captain, Pye stayed with his ship.

No sooner was Pye alone than the ghost appeared again. This time the image in black spoke. It said, "Be gone, you have no more to do here."

Frantically, Pye called to his crew members, who were making exceptionally good time getting clear of the distressed *Hopewell of London*. Fortunately, one of the nine in the small craft had been looking back toward Pye on the deck of the stranded ship. Although this man had said nothing to his mates, he had been watching the ship's leader ever since the group had begun to row away. He had clearly seen the phantom appear on the ship's deck, talk to the captain and then disappear. When he heard Pye calling and saw him waving at the men in the boat, he alerted the others and, within seconds, the rowboat was turned around to rescue the captain from his lone perch on the bridge of the apparently jinxed ship. Not long after Pye boarded the now-overcrowded rowboat, a passing ship picked up the frightened crew and their captain.

Had the ghost been a warning of impending danger or had this supernatural being caused the strange events? We can never know for certain, but Pye did add a comment that seems to verify that he had definitely stood side by side with a paranormal force.

"I had forgotten to express that one side of my face is burned and blasted sorely, which I felt within half an hour after I was gone out of the ship; but how it came upon me in the ship I could not tell being then in great horror and amazement."

He closed his report with the following words: "This is a true and perfect relation to the best of my knowledge in every respect and is attested to by nine men more, all belonging to my ship."

In closing, the man identified himself with his position, signing the document "John Pye, Master."

And so, it would seem that our interest in ghosts, their appearances and their effects on our lives is most certainly not a recent occurrence.

Ma Greene

Playing matchmaker can be risky, but when the match works out, the newly formed couple often remains grateful to their personal Cupid for years and years afterward. Mr. and Mrs. Mike Williams, for instance, hold Mary Becker Greene in high esteem because the elderly woman was integral to their first meeting in 1982. Ma Greene, as she was fondly known, accomplished this even though she had been dead for 43 years by that time.

The strange encounter occurred when the future Mrs. Williams (whom we'll call Judy) was the newly hired purser on the riverboat *Delta Queen*. During one of her first nights on the job, Judy heard noises that sounded like someone in pain. The new employee left her cabin to see if she could find the distressed person and be of any help to him or her. When Judy came to the door of cabin 109, she realized that the cries were coming from within. She knocked on the door before going into the room, where she found an elderly lady lying in bed. The poor old soul was complaining of being cold and feeling ill.

Although Judy had never met Mike Williams, the boat's first mate, she had been told that he had some medical training. So she went and found him.

"Please come quickly," Judy pleaded of Mike (also a pseudonym). "One of the passengers is not well."

Mike followed the purser back to cabin 109, but when they went in, no one was in the room. As a matter of fact, the place looked as if had been empty for some time.

Both young people were shocked by the sight of the empty room and stood staring silently for several minutes. Finally Mike recovered his voice and offered to walk Judy back to her room. As they made their way along the corridor, they passed a series of photographs.

"That's the lady I saw in the cabin," the young purser declared as she pointed to a picture hanging on a wall. It was a photo of Mary Becker Greene, the long-deceased former captain of the *Delta Queen*.

Fortunately, their puzzling experience that night had a happy ending. Mike and Judy were married months later and, to this day, they credit a ghost for having introduced them to one another. It wasn't until some-time later that they found out that cabin 109 was where Ma Greene had died.

That sighting of the ghost aboard the *Delta Queen* was somewhat unusual. For the most part, when the former captain's image is seen, she resembles Greene as she lived, not as she was dying.

Entertainers aboard the *Delta Queen* have often seen an apparition in a long, dark green housecoat. Phyllis Dale, a woman associated with the riverboat, recounted seeing the spirit walking along a passageway. The super-natural figure then disappeared before Dale's eyes.

When the ghost is spotted (often in her trademark green housecoat!), she's reported to be a very solid figure, apparently chatting with someone—someone invisible to those of this life.

A passenger who had been ill for a day of her voyage aboard the boat later thanked her traveling companion for comforting her by wiping her feverish brow so fre-quently during the day. She was not nearly so comforted when she was told that her friend had been off the river-boat on a shore excursion for the day. Nor when she real-ized that her friend did not own a green housecoat!

Other people have seen a woman dressed in the fashion of the 1930s float by them. Many of those witnesses presumed that the woman was alive and that she was lost. When they describe what they've seen to the *Delta Queen*'s crew, the reaction is, reassuringly, always the same. They are told: "Oh, that's just the spirit of Mary Becker Greene."

Although she does startle and surprise those seeing her for the first time, the ghost doesn't scare anyone who knows about her. Greene was one of the first female riverboat pilots, and she virtually lived for the *Delta Queen*. In death, she's known as a benevolent and even helpful spirit. Many employees claim they feel safer knowing that they're protected by her presence. Only once has the woman's ghost shown anger.

Throughout her long life, Mary Greene was greatly opposed to alcohol and refused to allow "spirits" to be served aboard her ship. Within weeks of Greene's death in 1949, her temperance dictate was overthrown and a bar was set up in the boat. Just seconds after the first ceremonial drink was poured, the *Delta Queen* was rammed by another river vessel—a barge named after Mary Becker Greene. Some might have thought this "accident" was quite a coincidence, but those who became aware of the hauntings thought otherwise.

When a crew from a television station came on board to film a story about the *Delta Queen*, the theory about a connection between ghostly presences and electric or electronic devices malfunctioning was well proven. And a cameraman had an experience he will likely never forget. The man aimed his camera at a wall of photographs and began to record their images—a simple and not very challenging assignment. Lingering for just a few seconds on each framed photo, he eventually came to a portrait of the late Captain Greene and began focusing on it. Suddenly he screamed, dropped the camera and fell to the floor.

The photographer's colleagues rushed to his side. They presumed that he'd had a heart attack. At first, the cameraman writhed in silent agony, then his lips began to move, but those gathered around heard nothing. The only way the fallen man could communicate at the time was to point at his camera.

Sometime later, when the photographer had calmed down sufficiently, he pointed to the picture of Ma Greene and blurted out, "She was alive!" For the balance of that assignment the photographer was withdrawn and silent and refused to be alone. What a shame that he wasn't able to realize that the ghost would never have done any harm to a person trying to preserve the *Delta Queen*—even if just in a photograph.

The *Delta Queen* is one of the Mississippi River's original riverboats, haunted, and perhaps in varying ways, preserved by one of the original characters of America's waterways.

It's Over

Some careers don't end well and that's always a shame. The following incident describes just such a case.

Tom Ellis had been a sailor since he was a youngster. In the early 1900s he worked as a deckhand on the *Eliza White,* a schooner that carried cargo to and from various ports in the Great Lakes. He loved the life of a sailor—the ships themselves, the adventure of it all, the challenge of facing the unpredictable weather conditions and even just the excitement of being on the water.

Ellis was a happy man the day his ship was moored at Hamilton, Ontario, on Lake Ontario. The rest of the crew,

While the Eliza White *was moored on Lake Ontario, a mysterious female phantom terrified Tom Ellis. He never sailed again.*

including the *Eliza White*'s captain, had gone ashore but Tom Ellis had no reason to do so. He passed the time sitting in his cabin reading and enjoying the solitude.

Suddenly he noticed he was getting uncomfortably cold. As he reached to pull a jacket down from a nearby hook, something in the periphery of his vision caught his attention. Tom Ellis gasped. There, standing in his cabin just a few feet from him, was the specter of a woman.

As soon as the image realized that the sailor had seen her, she began to walk toward him. She stopped, and at that moment Ellis knew for certain he was staring at the ghost of a woman in his shipboard cabin. Not only could the man see through the vision, but her clothes were pure white—too white to be of this earth. Worse, her eyes were as black as tiny beads of coal.

"She looked right at me," Tom Ellis later attested. "I have never seen such horror and terror and fear and pain in anyone's eyes as I did in hers. She was wringing her hands as though in agony."

Tom Ellis bolted from his cabin and fled from the ship. As he ran across the dock and toward the street, he saw his former mates returning to the vessel. Ellis yelled, "I quit. I'll never sail again." And he never did. The man's long and proud career as a sailor was over.

Even today we do not know whose ghost he saw that day. We do know that he was neither a drinking man nor a man prone to flights of fancy, and that all who knew him believed that he had, that day, seen a dreadful ghost. We don't know who the ghost could have been, whether she was connected in some way to the *Eliza White* or Ellis himself, or perhaps was just a lost soul drifting through. Fortunately, we do know that the *Eliza White* and the rest of her crew went on to make many successful voyages together. Presumably, no matter how frightening she was, the ghost was not a harbinger of ill.

The only real victim of the ghost sighting was Tom Ellis' career. It was finished, and certainly not on a positive note.

An Enormous Disaster

The *Great Eastern* was a haunted and doomed vessel even before she had sailed a mile.

Among the many seagoing superstitions is a belief that changing a ship's name will bring bad luck. But superstitions are just silliness, aren't they? Perhaps you might want to read about this jinxed and possessed giant before making up your mind.

On a chilly, gray day early in November 1857, workers and dignitaries gathered at an English dockyard to watch history being made. The largest ship ever built, the *Leviathan*, which later was named the *Great Eastern*, was about to be launched. The woman selected to christen the gargantuan vessel was a daughter of the man who owned the Hope diamond. She swung the bottle of champagne toward the hull in time-honored tradition.

Isambard Kingdom Brunel was the man behind the design and manufacture of this engineering masterpiece. The ship had a potential speed of 14 knots, was 690 feet long and weighed in at approximately 20,000 tons. Hence, her name was well chosen. Unfortunately no shipyard of that time was capable of moving this colossus into the sea in a normal stern-first manner. It was proposed, therefore, that the ship be launched sideways—a plan that didn't work any better in reality than one might have imagined it would. The job was painstakingly slow. It took three months to accomplish. Worse, it also cost two lives.

As a result, the *Leviathan*'s launch, which began in November 1857, was not completed until January 30, 1858. Many of the witnesses to the final portion of that

Passengers on the hapless Leviathan *heard inexplicable banging sounds from the hull—likely the work of two angry worker spirits.*

tedious project soon became sorry that they'd attended. The gallery built for the spectators to stand on collapsed under their weight, and hundreds of people were thrown to the ground below. No one died, but many men, women and children were seriously injured.

Damage during the launch was even more extensive than that. The wave that the *Leviathan* made when it hit the water was so huge that dozens of vessels in the waters nearby were swamped and sunk.

The cost involved in this painfully long process of launching the ship eventually forced the ship's owners into receivership, which left the *Leviathan* abandoned at the dock before she'd sailed a mile. The hulk rested uneasily there for a year. Finally, the Great Ship Company bought her, changed her name to the *Great Eastern* and she was sea-ready by August 1859.

She was also haunted. Rumor had it that during initial construction of the ship's gigantic hull, a worker (and perhaps his apprentice, too) had somehow been sealed alive into what was effectively a tomb, between two layers of steel.

Despite all that had gone wrong up to this point, the *Great Eastern* was eventually ready to begin her first test voyage. Not long into that trial, an explosion occurred in the engine room. The reverberations were so strong that most of the glass in the ship was shattered. Five sailors died instantly in the blast. A sixth drowned when he threw himself overboard in an attempt to extinguish the flames that engulfed his body.

Just before the ship's first trip across the Atlantic Ocean from the British Isles to North America, the *Great Eastern*'s crew mutinied. The shipping company took the workers to court and won the case against the sailors, but many of the men were sentenced to jail, so the company was forced to recruit new employees. By then, word had spread about the bad luck that seemed to follow this ship, and reliable sailors were not eager to sign on—especially not for this, the ship's first trans-Atlantic voyage.

While both legal and hiring battles were being waged on land, the ship broke away from her dockside moorings and began to float aimlessly. This situation proved dangerous not only for the *Great Eastern*, but also for the ships nearby. After a Herculean effort by many experienced sailors, the giant ship was finally tethered. During the cleanup process from this mishap, one of the huge ship's auxiliary boats sunk—with two men and a boy on board. All drowned.

Still, the ship's owners pressed on and sailed on. Tremendous excitement was generated in North America about the floating giant crossing the ocean. Eight different cities vied for the right to welcome her. New York City won. A reporter with the *New York Times* wrote that there hadn't been so much "worldwide interest in any craft since Noah's Ark."

As the ship left the English dock, engineer Brunel stood watching while having his photograph taken. Seconds later he collapsed and died.

In keeping with what everyone was sure Brunel would have wanted, the unprofitable voyage was not postponed. During the journey, many of the 35 passengers (the *Great Eastern* could have carried 4000) and 418 crew members reported hearing strange knocking sounds. Those aboard said that the noises seemed to be coming from the hull and sounded like a hammer banging on steel. Investigations failed to turn up any possible source for the sounds.

When the *Great Eastern*'s sails were set and the engines stopped, the captain realized that, as a result of a critical calculation error made during the planning and design process, the ship would never move without engine power. He ordered the engines restarted, but the throttles were jammed and, for three days, the ship and all aboard her bobbed helplessly in the Atlantic Ocean. During those comparatively quiet days, everyone aboard became well aware of the phantom banging sounds emanating from below deck.

Once the ship was moving again, and for no reason anyone was ever able to discern, a cook went completely mad and began to run throughout the ship with a knife, threatening whoever was in his path. Fortunately, he was caught and subdued before he hurt anyone.

Still, the banging sounds continued.

As the ship pulled into New York harbor, she was greeted by a great crowd—a crowd that included a condemned man. At the convict's request, his execution had been delayed long enough for him to see the *Great Eastern* approaching. Minutes after she appeared, a hood was placed over the doomed man's head and he became the last soul in North America to be hanged for piracy.

Aboard the *Great Eastern*, the banging sounds were muffled by the welcoming roar from the shore. As the giant docked amid the celebrations, she hit the wharf and damaged both the ship and the dock.

Once the ship was lashed in place, customs inspectors boarded. As soon as they did, they heard the strange banging sounds that those aboard had been hearing for the entire trip. The customs officers, sure that there was a stowaway, searched the vessel from bow to stern, but found nothing out of the ordinary.

As the *Great Eastern* sat in the harbor, a fire broke out very close to the ship. Both the New York City Fire Department and the Harbor Authority Fire Department were called. An argument between the two forces over who had the right to extinguish the blaze escalated into a riot.

Although no one was killed, firefighters shot, clubbed and axed one another while the sailors aboard the *Great Eastern* put out the fire.

Not long after the *Great Eastern* left New York, she collided with another vessel, nearly sinking the smaller one. Other than that, the trip was uneventful—aside from the persistent knocking sounds that everyone heard.

The *Great Eastern*'s second attempt to sail from England to North America was even less successful then her first. Barely out of British waters, she was hit by a gale and damaged so badly that she had to turn back. More than 100 people were injured in that incident. All had heard the banging sounds.

Once she was refitted, the ship once again sailed to New York—where she hit a submerged rock, which has ever since been called Great Eastern Rock. While repairs were being made, the workers decided that the banging sounds they were hearing were caused by a loose part. Despite intensive efforts, however, no loose part was ever found.

By 1863, the ship's second owner was also forced into bankruptcy. The *Great Eastern* fell into the hands of a company that thought it could definitely benefit from the ship's enormous size because this company was responsible for laying cable across the Atlantic Ocean. At first all went well, but after uncoiling more than 1200 miles (1920 kilometers) of cable, workers neglected to splice the cable where it was required. The cable broke, and as a result, all their efforts to that point had been for naught. They had to start again. By July 27, 1866, the cable laying was successfully completed. Most of the sailors aboard the *Great Eastern* were very glad to see the end of that assignment because the frequent banging sounds from the ship's hull were hard on everyone's nerves.

The following year, the *Great Eastern* changed ownership for a third time and once again carried passengers—including science fiction author Jules Verne. Verne and roughly 200 others sailed from England to France en route to the 1867 Paris Exposition. All aboard heard the bangs from below.

Shortly after that trip, the new owners went bankrupt, and the *Great Eastern* was sold for scrap. Wrecking crews hurried as fast as they could to get their work done because they were unnerved by banging sounds echoing from the hull area, but the wrecking process was still extremely time consuming because the ship was so large.

When the scrap workers reached the point of dismantling the huge hull, they finally found the explanation for the banging sounds. Between the two layers of hull at the bow of the ship were not just one, some say, but two skeletons—one of a man and one of a boy—as well as an array of rusty old tools. An unfortunate worker and his apprentice had apparently been sealed alive in a floating tomb.

At least when the ship was being destroyed once and for all, a reason for the banging sounds and all the bad luck was found. The *Leviathan/Great Eastern* had been haunted by two very angry spirits for her entire career.

Dead Aboard

Did you read that amazing article in *Harper's* magazine? Apparently during a fierce gale, the *Hascall*, a fishing schooner docked off the coast of Maine, broke loose from her tethers. She rammed another craft, the *Andrew Johnson*, with such force that she sank her. What was worse, though, was that the sailors aboard the *Hascall* didn't even stop to offer assistance to those they'd put in such terrible peril. Not one of the *Hascall's* crew made any attempt to even slow their ship, let alone to help the victims. As a result, all hands on the *Andrew Johnson* went down with their ship.

That immutable law of karma immediately took its toll on the heartless crew of the *Hascall*. That very night, when all her sailors were in town, people near the docks reported seeing strange lights floating around her decks. As more and more people stopped to observe the eerie phenomenon, the group gathered was treated to quite a spectacular supernatural display.

One after another, images of sailors appeared on deck. According to the write-up in the magazine, witnesses stated that each entity would seem to reach over the ship's side and pull in a fishing net before disappearing from view, only to be replaced by another vision that did exactly the same thing.

This bizarre activity eventually attracted quite an audience until the witnesses included people related to the crew lost on the *Andrew Johnson*. Those poor folks were shocked beyond belief, for, as they watched, the ghosts of their recently deceased relatives finished pulling up invisible fishing nets and then, one at a time, each of the specters climbed over the side of the *Hascall*.

Moments later the haunting was no longer visible, but the crowd could hear the eerie sound of oars dipping in and out of the water. The gathering of ghosts had apparently boarded rowboats, and all the phantoms were making their way to the hereafter.

No one ever sailed aboard the haunted *Hascall* again.

If you want to read the original report yourself, you can find it in *Harper's* magazine—the September 1880 issue.

Official Exorcism

Many people who experience a haunting do so in fearful isolation. They would rather shiver in silence than risk having people think that they have lost their minds. This hesitancy means that it could take years for a ghost story to become public. Other times, the truth comes out rather more quickly, but only through a series of strange events. The following is one that required an extremely unusual and unlikely set of circumstances to occur before the story could become a matter of public record.

Employment authorities in Bridlington, England, noticed that a group of sailors, the crew from a particular fishing vessel, frequently drew unemployment benefits from a government fund. Immediately after this pattern was noticed, investigators were assigned to examine the situation.

All the out-of-work fishermen had crewed for a skipper named Derek Gates aboard his trawler, the *Pickering*. And, when they were interviewed, they all told exactly the same story, that, although the pay was good and their workmates trustworthy, they hated to work on the boat because they were sure there was a ghost on board with them.

It's not likely that British civil servants had ever before heard such an explanation for frequent unemployment. They must have puzzled for some time over how to handle this situation. They decided that first they needed more information, so the investigators went back to interview Gates and his sailors again. The sailors described nights at sea when the boat's radar would dangerously malfunction. In addition, they maintained that the boat's steering would sometimes be impossible to control, that temperatures below deck would drop many degrees in some spots but not in others, and that lights would turn off or on when no one was near either the lights or the switches that controlled them.

One of the members of the investigating committee was apparently knowledgeable about ghosts, and he quickly recognized that the men were describing the classic signs of a haunting. Another member of the committee was fascinated by the history of ships and, after doing research, discovered some interesting facts about the *Pickering*. It seemed that the vessel the crew now claimed was haunted had once flown under the flag of Ireland. During that time, a sailor had been washed overboard and his body had never been recovered. Almost immediately after that accident, the boat had been sold. The investigators decided that this sailor was likely haunting the ship.

When the government investigators reconvened, they decided that the only way to keep the crew of the *Pickering* gainfully employed was to exorcise the long-ago drowned sailor's ghostly soul from the craft. They called in an Anglican minister named Tom Willis, who sprinkled holy water throughout the trawler while praying for the presence to move on to its afterlife.

Derek Gates later reported to Reuter's News Agency that as soon as Willis had finished performing the ritual, the atmosphere in his boat changed from menacingly haunted to "warm and friendly." Not once since then has the entire crew of the *Pickering* been unemployed at the same time. As a matter of fact, Gates told the reporter that since the minister's blessing, the fishing vessel is "having very successful catches."

Perhaps this was one time when the government really was there to help. And what time was that? Well, the story was reported in the *Calgary Herald* on December 15, 1987. As no new reports have been filed since that time, we can probably assume that the deceased spirit is now at peace and that Derek Gates and the crew of the *Pickering* have worked—in peace and plenty—ever since.

Fateful Vision

There are omens aplenty in the seafaring world. One of the most deeply entrenched beliefs is that if a ghost is seen aboard a ship, that vessel is doomed. When stories circulate that a craft is haunted, few sailors will serve on that ship. Sometimes, such a situation eventually leads to the destruction of a ship that is otherwise in excellent shape and is completely seaworthy. The following incident is an example of such a misfortune.

The name of this particular vessel was the *Pontiac*. Her home port was Liverpool, England, and until July 1863, she sailed from there to various South American cities on a regular basis. For several years, these voyages went well. Prior to one return trip, however, the captain realized that the size of his crew had dwindled and that he would need to hire more men before heading home. He scouted the docks of Callao, Peru, where he was moored, until he found three men he trusted who welcomed the opportunity to earn some money. After that matter had been attended to, the captain was sure the voyage home was going to be a good one.

Unfortunately, the following days and nights at sea proved the man's feelings about the trip were as wrong as they could possibly have been. One clear, starlit night, as most of the men slept, two of the *Pontiac's* most experienced sailors were in charge of guiding the craft on its route back home. One man, William, was on a routine patrol of the decks when Edmund, the man at the wheel, let out a bloodcurdling scream.

Abruptly abandoning his patrol, William ran as fast as he dared to his mate's side. Before he had a chance to ask what the matter was, Edmund began shouting, "There's a man, there's a man on the boat!"

William looked in the direction of Edmund's gaze but saw nothing unusual, certainly nothing worthy of such a shriek. William wondered for a moment if he had become the brunt of some sort of a joke.

"Of course there's a man on the ship. There are lots of men on this ship. There are even three new men on this homeward voyage that were not on the outbound trip. They're the rest of the crew. You know that full well, Edmund," William teased, thinking he was playing along with the other man's attempt at humor.

"Will, this was not any of the crew that I saw. This was a terrible phantom. He stood in front of me, about a yard above the deck and just stared. His eyes were not normal. They were like coals aflame with evil," Edmund described shakily.

After hearing those words and the pained tone in which they were spoken, Edmund no longer wondered if he was being taken in by his colleague's warped sense of humor. He knew for a fact that a depraved spirit had visited the boat. Both Edmund and William also knew what a terrible portent that was, especially as the vision was a robed and hooded figure without a face—except for two coals of burning, orange flames where, if the image had been human, the eyes should have been. That meant only one thing—the phantom was a death's head. Evil would follow.

Their cries and loud conversation had pierced the silent night and awakened most of their seagoing colleagues.

Within seconds, word of the sighting spread from crew member to crew member.

The ensuing chaos had just begun to settle down when the youngest of the crew felt a hand on his shoulder. Slowly, the boy turned around. If he'd been hoping to see one of his older mates attempting to calm him, he must have been terribly disappointed because there, staring at him intently, was a tall, hooded form. The lad tried to cry out, but he was mute from fear. He could only stand in silent terror as he watched the evil-looking manifestation move about before pushing the hood of its long robe back. All the boy could make out clearly was the eerie illumination from the glowing orange orbs.

Just as the boy's panic was about to reach unstoppable heights, the ghost evaporated into the cold sea air.

After two more blissfully uneventful days and nights at sea, the *Pontiac* moored at the port of Liverpool. Never had any of those aboard seen such a welcome sight. They had survived the voyage—a journey that had seemed fatefully doomed by supernatural forces.

As soon as they had the *Pontiac*'s mooring ropes secured on the pier, the men fled from the ship—never to return. Within days, every seaman for miles around knew of the death ghost that had visited the *Pontiac*. No matter how hard he tried, or how much pay he offered, the ship's captain was never again able to attract another crew to sail the *Pontiac*.

She sat dockside for months before her owners gave up and demolished their almost-new vessel. They sold the lumber they were able to salvage, hopefully not to another shipbuilder, for spirits have often been known to become embedded in the materials in a haunted place.

As we don't know for certain if that meant the end of the robed and hooded vision with the evil eyes, it's possible that the haunting continued on another ship or even several other ships. Possibly even the mast of the ship reported in the documented news report that follows.

A Newspaper Report

In March 1885, a lake-going vessel with a veteran crew left her home harbor near Chicago, Illinois, destined for Buffalo, New York. Two sailors, one whose name has been lost in the mists of time and another whose name was Bill, had climbed to the topmost mast of the ship to repair a potential problem. Within seconds of one another, both sailors fell to the ship's deck. Both died instantly.

From that moment on, it was widely believed that the ghosts of those two sailors haunted that ship. As is typical in such cases, the ship's owners found it more and more difficult to find a worthy crew to sail her, for most sailors had heard about the tragedy and the subsequent haunting. Most seamen wanted nothing to do with a ship that was haunted by the souls of their deceased colleagues. They considered such a haunted craft to be a "Jonah," an unlucky ship with a portent of ill.

Perhaps because this accidental haunting occurred during Victorian times when interest in the paranormal generally, and ghosts in particular, was very high, news about the ghosts was even reported, in detail, by at least

If sailors die on board a ship, she often becomes cursed.

one newspaper. The *Chicago Times* ran the following prominently placed article in March 1885.

On its arrival at Buffalo, New York, the men [from the ship] went on shore as soon as they were paid off. They said the ship had lost her luck. The story got round and some…refused to work on her. Even the mate was affected by it. At last she got ready to sail for Cleveland where we were to load coal.

The captain managed to get a crew by going to a crimp [press-gang operator] who ran sailors in…They came on board two-thirds drunk and the mate was steering them into the forecastle when one of them stopped and said, pointing aloft, "What have you got a figurehead on the mast for?" The mate looked up and then turned pale, "It's Bill," he said, and with that the whole lot jumped onto the dock. One sailor said that he had not seen anything unusual. The mate, however, told the captain to look for another officer to replace him. The captain was so much affected that he put some men on another schooner and then hired a new crew before sailing for Cleveland. They never got there. They were sunk en route by a steamer.

Had a dreadful self-fulfilling prophecy brought about the accident by forcing the captain to choose less and less qualified help, help that was unable to save the ship? Or had the ghost, which had so startled the two men that they had fallen to their deaths, actually appeared to warn those aboard that they were sailing on a doomed vessel?

Or perhaps the owner of this ship had purchased some of the timber to build her from a scrap dealer in Liverpool, scrap that came from the *Pontiac*. We can only wonder and guess.

A Living Image

We hear a great deal about the strange events in the myste-
rious vortex known as the Bermuda Triangle. But there are
seafaring ghost stories associated with Bermuda that are
not in any way connected to the Triangle. The next true tale
is one of those.

☠

In 1828, Donald McPhee Lee founded the *Royal Gazette*,
a Bermuda newspaper. Starting such an enterprise, especially back then, was a difficult undertaking. The job
began with a voyage to Halifax, Nova Scotia, in 1825
where Lee purchased a printing press and other equipment that would be required to start the newspaper he
envisioned.

Lee decided to ship his recent investments home
aboard the *Sally Ann*, a Bermudian schooner owned by
postmaster James Taylor. The voyage would be led by
Captain Phalan, a well-experienced sailor. And so, with a
crew of six, one passenger in addition to Lee, a shipment
of pork, corn and potatoes, as well as the enormous printing press and related equipment, the vessel prepared for a
routine sail south.

Captain Phalan delayed the *Sally Ann*'s departure until
Saturday, even though they were cleared by port authorities to sail on Friday. Phalan was respecting the long-held
naval superstition that bad luck follows a sail that begins
on Friday—the day many believe Christ was crucified.
Lee, not being a seafaring man but a man of commercial

Stranded in the middle of the ocean, the Sally Ann *required supernatural aid to guide her home.*

interests, was annoyed at this seeming waste of time, but as the captain was clearly in command, there was little the future publisher could do but to wait as patiently as he could for their departure.

As it turned out, the captain's caution actually caused, rather than prevented, terrible and tragic trouble. Leaving Halifax on Saturday, October 29, 1825, put the *Sally Ann* and all aboard her into an horrendous gale as the craft approached the Gulf Stream. Severe winds threw the small craft many miles off course. When the weather subsided and Phalan regained control of his ship, he calculated a new course and continued the journey.

Phalan's calculations must have been seriously inaccurate at some point, because his navigational instructions actually took the *Sally Ann*, its crew, passengers and cargo, farther away from their destination. Soon, everyone on board realized that they were in potential peril. The captain however, was too proud to hoist distress signals. And so, after a short respite, the *Sally Ann* bobbed about in the waves like a doomed cork.

When those aboard—the crew and both passengers—threatened violence if the captain did not act more responsibly, Phalan finally agreed to signal for help. Still, days went by and no other ship approached the struggling *Sally Ann*. It was then that a sailor realized that the vessel was painted the same colors as the ships used by some currently active and especially dangerous pirates. The *Sally Ann* and all aboard her were doomed because no reasonable mariner would ever come near that vessel. Water and food supplies were dangerously low and morale was even lower. Worse, there was no hope in sight.

Then, without warning, a wind began to blow. The air currents became stronger and stronger, creating huge waves that buffeted the already stressed craft, its passengers and its cargo. Two sailors caught on deck were swept off the ship and out to sea before being hurled back onto the deck by the same wave that had abducted them just seconds before.

The frightened sailors ran below deck to report the ter-
rifying incident to Phalan. They found him in his cabin—
suddenly and inexplicably blind. As a consequence of
the captain's disability, Donald Lee, on the ship only to
accompany his printing equipment, was suddenly forced
to take over the responsibility of sailing the *Sally Ann*.

Starting this voyage on a Saturday had proven to be
the worst decision Captain Phalan had ever made.

Although Phalan was blind and had put many lives in
jeopardy, personal vanity and pride still ruled his deci-
sions. When a mate spotted another vessel on the horizon,
the commander forbade anyone from attempting to make
contact with it. If word got back that a ship under his
supervision had been found in such serious distress,
Captain Phalan knew his career would be ruined. His ego
dictated that he cause further risk to his own life and
those he had been entrusted to transport rather than ask
for badly needed help.

Lee, fearing for his life, did the best he could at the
wheel of the *Sally Ann* but, finally, after more than 24
hours of intense concentration, he succumbed to exhaustion and collapsed on his bunk. In the few seconds that
passed before the man lost consciousness, he saw an
image—the image of a close friend—appear before him.

The apparition was the ghost of a well-respected man
and close friend of Lee's. He smiled at Donald Lee and
said to him quietly, "Do not despair. You will reach
Bermuda safely." The vision then vaporized before his
eyes. Lee was so shaken by this strange encounter that just
before falling into a deep sleep, he noted the exact time
that the apparition had appeared to him.

Several weeks later, her hull barely seaworthy, those on board barely alive, the beleaguered *Sally Ann* found the safety of her home port. The vision that had spoken to Lee had apparently been accurate in his prediction. Everyone lived to tell about the dreadful adventure. And, when they started to share information about the nearly fatal voyage, the crew revealed that they had been so insanely maddened by the hopelessness of their situation that they had been ready to murder Lee in his bunk. But as they had approached his room with murder on their minds, they had been confronted with an unnaturally cold force of air that had blocked their passage.

This strange encounter occurred at exactly the same moment that the spirit of Donald Lee's friend had appeared to the exhausted man lying in his bunk. To make this strange tale even stranger, the spirit could not have been a ghost in the usual sense of the word, for the man who offered the comforting and accurate words to Lee was still very much alive and living in Glasgow, Scotland. Lee's vision of this friend must have been a result of astral projection by the Scotsman.

Despite all the threats to its very existence, the first issue of Bermuda's *Royal Gazette* rolled off the presses on January 8, 1828. The newspaper continues to publish to this day. Not many commercial enterprises enjoy such longevity, perhaps because not many commercial enterprises are aided by a supernatural force.

Ghostly Guardians

Occasionally, we read about a single sailor in a small craft trying to make some Herculean voyage. Bob Fowler of Florida was just such an adventurer. In the summer of 1978, he readied himself and his 18-foot sailboat, the *Miskeeter*, for a trans-Atlantic crossing. If this voyage went well, Fowler then intended to sail the *Miskeeter* around the globe.

The day Fowler left on his voyage, all looked as if it would go well for him. The day was sunny and clear, the seas were as calm as one can ever expect the Atlantic Ocean to be. That night, however, conditions changed dramatically and Fowler was in danger. Winds and waves buffeted his tiny craft about. Despite his skill as a sailor and his best efforts, Fowler was no match for the storm's power. There was nothing he could do but pray and hope that, by some miracle, his life would be spared.

Day after day, the storm persisted. Fowler was exhausted. The gales were so fierce that even larger ships couldn't make their way through the storm to rescue Fowler and the *Miskeeter*.

A terrible resignation came over Bob Fowler. There was absolutely nothing he could do but try to stay alive until his circumstances improved substantially. He strapped himself into his bunk and waited, having no idea which breath would be his last.

Fortunately, the beaten sailor soon lost consciousness. According to the report he gave later, he "had been awake for 90 [consecutive] hours." Some period of time later, Fowler's sleep was disturbed by the sounds of voices in his cabin. Fowler could not figure out what was going on.

On the advice of a ghostly sailor, Bob Fowler shot a flare into the sky to attract help. He was rescued shortly thereafter.

He opened his eyes and saw three men in his cabin. They were dressed as though they belonged on the wharf of an exclusive yacht club.

Telling himself that he was merely hallucinating from fear, exhaustion, hunger and thirst, Fowler closed his eyes again and turned his face toward the wall. As he did, an extremely rational thought came to the forefront of his mind. Four people, himself on his bunk as well as his three strange visitors, could not possibly fit into the cabin aboard his sailboat. When he realized that, he knew for certain that his mind was creating fantasies.

Despite this reasonable conclusion, the three men—whether they were imaginary or not—were engaged in a deep conversation with one another.

"Should we lay ahull?" said one. Those words were followed by, "Should we run with or without warps?"

"Don't run."

"She's too short. She'll pitch."

On and on these strangers talked, apparently trying to decide how best to help Bob Fowler. The trio seemed to be in firm agreement on one matter though—that Fowler was not able to save his own life. The insult came through loud and clear to the nearly delirious man in the bunk. He tried not to care, continuing to tell himself that these images were not real but the imagined consequences of the situation he was in.

As time wore on, this skeptical attitude became more and more difficult for Fowler to hang on to, for these illusions were now rousing him and giving him directions to tend to different parts of his sloop. Fighting to remain conscious, Fowler wondered what the biggest enemy was at this point—the storm or the strange commandeering intruders.

After performing each supernaturally assigned chore, Fowler would collapse on his bunk again, utterly exhausted.

Finally, one of the three sailors appeared and ordered the ship's owner to get out on deck.

"Fire your flare gun. There's a ship nearby that can save you."

Barely able to move, Bob Fowler drew on strength he didn't know he had and made his way up top. Before falling into a heap he shot half a dozen flares into the sky. His efforts were rewarded when a freighter suddenly veered into sight.

Seconds later, all reserves drained, Fowler slowly made his way back to his cabin. The three strangers were gone. Soon after that, the *Miskeeter* and its owner were rescued and taken safely into port by the ship he'd alerted with the flare gun.

When he was interviewed several months after the incident, Bob Fowler was once again holding to his skepticism even though there were many problems with the logic. For example, if he was correct in believing that his mind conjured up those experienced men of the sea, then how did he know exactly when to struggle to the deck and fire the flares?

The answer to this seagoing mystery is certainly a paranormal one, for either supernatural beings directed Fowler or he psychically perceived that a potential rescue ship was nearby. Either answer poses a challenge to a skeptical mind. Fowler's continued skepticism offers evidence of either tenacity or stubbornness.

Ghost Brothers

Friday, November 13, 1942. In the South Pacific, the night was inky black, ominous and deadly. The wrath of World War II raged hideously throughout the world. One of the longest, ugliest and most lethal naval battles of the entire war, the Battle of Guadalcanal, thundered across the waves. By the battle's end, only five of the American ships involved remained intact.

One of those was USS *Juneau*, carrying 700 young sailors. The complement included five brothers: Joseph, Francis, Albert, Madison and George Sullivan. All the men, the Sullivans among them, were thankful to have escaped the battle alive. By the time the captain shouted the order that started the *Juneau* on her way to safe harbor, the atmosphere aboard the light carrier was one of both exhaustion and relief.

The tensions and stresses from the horrible battle had barely begun to drain out of the sailors' bodies when an enemy torpedo pierced the *Juneau*'s hull. The ship sank in minutes. Only 10 men survived. Mr. and Mrs. Sullivan's five beloved sons were not among that number.

The deceased Sullivan brothers soon became a symbol of all who died on that dreadful Friday the 13th. To honor those lives, USS *The Sullivans* was built and launched in time to serve during the last years of the war. Not only was her name an exceptional one—ships named in the plural are very rare—but her colors were also unusual. Her name was emblazoned in bright green, and a shamrock painted on her hull further testified to the brothers' Irish roots.

After the end of the war, *The Sullivans* and many like her were retired. Except for periodic checks, these moth-balled ships were essentially abandoned. As federally owned property, however, some monitoring had to be conducted. According to Adi-Kent Jeffrey, author of *Ghosts in the Valley*, during the early 1970s, when an electrician's commanding officer ordered the enlisted man to go on board *The Sullivans*, "he did that which is never done. He refused." That man had heard that the ghosts of Joseph, Francis, Albert, Madison and George Sullivan roamed the passageways of the ship named for them. The date when this frightened electrician refused to obey an order was Friday the 13th, the sun had already set and the night was as black as it had been on that fateful night of Friday, November 13, 1942. Nothing could have made the sailor board that vessel.

After some searching, the commander did find an electrician either brave or naïve enough to board the rusting craft. The man soon discovered that he was not going to enjoy this assignment. He had been at work for only a few minutes when his toolbox vanished from his side. He finished the work as best he could but never boarded the ship again.

The electricians' mates supported their frightened colleagues fully, for they, too, had heard that dockyard workers serving the port where the hulk rested had reported seeing lights flickering throughout *The Sullivans*, even though power to the ship had been cut off long before. Others sent to do work on those haunted decks fled after seeing five luminous shapes floating about in the darkened corridors. As well, disembodied sounds of moaning and groaning have caused others to leave the phantoms of the five Sullivan brothers alone in their eternal agony.

And so, the haunted ship USS *The Sullivans* has certainly fulfilled one of its purposes. No one who knows about her haunted shell can ever forget the terrible tragedy of the Battle of Guadalcanal.

The Most Famous Ship of All

One of the most famous, and infamous, of all the world's sailings began on April 10, 1912, at the port of Southampton, England.

While hundreds of people gathered on the dock to bid farewell to friends or relatives boarding the luxurious ocean liner, thousands of others were there simply to witness the history-making event. The *Titanic*, that most opulent of all ships, was about to set out on her maiden voyage with a well-trained crew, a capable staff and 2227 eager passengers.

Over the 100-plus years since the enormous ship sank, taking 1522 souls with her to a frigid watery grave at the bottom of the North Atlantic, something of a small industry has built up around the *Titanic*. Books, films, websites, clubs and more have been created to answer our fascination with the ship's poignant legacy.

By now, the *Titanic* even has her own cache of folklore. For a retelling of some of those legends, please see my book *Canadian Ghost Stories* (Lone Pine Publishing, 2001). For our purposes in this book, however, we will deal with some of the less well-known spooky stories that swirl around the nautical graveyard.

Many ghost stories are told about the ill-fated HMS Titanic.

One of the most puzzling and poignant stories associated with the *Titanic* disaster occurred, oddly enough, in landlocked Winnipeg, Manitoba, on the Canadian Prairies.

Charles Morgan was the minister at Rosedale Methodist Church in Winnipeg at the time. He was a very dedicated man and it was his habit to remain at the church most of the day each Sunday. Several hours before the last service of the day on Sunday, April 14, 1912, Morgan posted the numbers of the hymns to be sung, then he sat down to relax and meditate.

He drifted into a mental state something like a trance, and twice saw the same number flash before his eyes. It seemed to be the number of a certain hymn, but one he was not familiar with. At the end of the service, he called out this number, something he had never done before, and the congregation all struggled through the singing of a hymn unfamiliar to them.

Amazingly, the words of that hymn, the number of which had come to Charles Morgan while he was meditating, are "Hear us Father while we pray to Thee for those in peril on the sea."

Within a few days, it became common knowledge that the congregation sang that prayer just about the time when a young minister aboard the *Titanic* was conducting a last sing-along in the ship's lounge. Too bad we have no way of knowing whether or not the doomed passengers aboard the sinking ship had been singing that very hymn at the moment that Reverend Morgan had telepathically received the encouragement to add one more, very specific, hymn to the service he was about to conduct.

There have also been cases where possible reincarnations have been linked to the *Titanic*. For instance, Donald Brown was born in Illinois on August 29, 1960. He was only four days old and about to be given his first bath, when he initially demonstrated his great aversion to water. That terribly negative reaction didn't leave Donald for years. He was terrified of water. His mother was puzzled. None of her other children had ever shown such a fear. Stranger still, as Donald grew from a baby into a child, he

Gravestones of Titanic *victims in Fairview Lawn Cemetery in Halifax*

showed no hesitancy in joining his friends in any risk-taking games. Water seemed to be his only fear.

Donald was about six years old when he first heard of the awful tragedy of the *Titanic*. The child seemed so fascinated by everything to do with the ship and its sinking that his uncle bought him a book about the subject. This was a book that one would not normally choose for a child this young but, nevertheless, little Donald didn't just read the book—he studied it. By the time the child was seven years old, he was an expert on all aspects of the giant ship. He had memorized passenger lists, knew the numbers and capacity of lifeboats carried during her fateful maiden voyage, the mechanics that went into building her and even the music that was played as the ship sank.

Donald's depth of knowledge and emotional involvement with the then 50-year-old tragedy became a concern to his parents. He spoke with great fondness of two little children who used to enjoy playing in an empty room they'd discovered below the ship's main deck. He also told his parents about the dreadful cries of people as they jumped, or fell, overboard into the icy waters—and to certain death. During these recitations, Donald would become visibly upset.

Then he began to describe the horrors of being in the North Atlantic—of how the people would choke and cough when the cold, salty water splashed into their mouths. Often, Donald would end one of these one-sided conversations by wailing, "There should have been more lifeboats."

When Donald reached adolescence, his fear of water was still very much a part of him. Then the family's next-door neighbors had a swimming pool installed in their yard. Slowly, Donald began to make use of the owner's open invitation for the Browns to enjoy this new facility. Over the next few years, Donald actually learned how to get himself from one side of the pool to the other. He was not a strong or skilled swimmer, but he'd certainly come a long way from the kid who'd been terrified of water.

In July 1980, the month before Donald would have turned 20, he and some friends went camping near a quarry. Donald decided to cool off in the water. He was not far from shore and was swimming along without any problem when one of his friends on the shore called out to him, "It's 30 feet deep there, you know!"

No sooner were the words spoken than Donald panicked, began thrashing about and, seconds later, drowned.

At his memorial service, Donald's mother requested that the hymn *Nearer My God To Thee* be played. That was the hymn that the orchestra aboard the *Titanic* was playing as the giant slid beneath the surface of the water.

Sometime after Donald's death, Mrs. Brown was watching a television show about the *Titanic*. An elderly woman, one of the few remaining survivors of the disaster, was being interviewed. She told the show's host that she and her little brother "used to play all day in an empty room." Her statement was almost word for word the same as what Donald had once told his mother years before. The elderly survivor also told of the horrors of listening to people screaming and choking as they hit the frigid seawater. Again, her description was nearly identical to what young Donald had said. Perhaps his reincarnated soul had been giving a firsthand account of that dreadful night.

Will the eerie stories surrounding this one terrible sea tragedy ever end? They may not. For instance, when the remains of the *Titanic* were found 73 years later in her own burial ground, the ship was lying aligned in the same direction as were the victims' bodies, which had been buried in Fairview Lawn Cemetery, Halifax, Nova Scotia.

In 2001, when a traveling display about the doomed liner arrived for exhibition in Chile, the organizer told news reporters, "Guards, visitors and even the police have all reported experiencing strange phenomena such as seeing apparitions" around various artifacts from the *Titanic*. These ghost sightings included the clear image of a woman dressed in a long white dress typical of clothes from the early 1900s.

The guards at the museum hosting the show often heard "human voices and footsteps" coming from the display area when they knew for certain that no one was anywhere near it. This was not much of a surprise to the exhibition's organizers because they had heard the same reports when their show was in Argentina. It seemed that the psychic energy associated with the items was still strong enough to reach out across time from their plane to ours.

Interestingly, these horrors have not stopped shipping lines from naming additions to their fleets with monikers similar to the word "Titanic." Even the White Star Line was brave enough to name a huge passenger ship the *Teutonic*. That ship limped to harbor at New York City after hitting an iceberg. And a cargo vessel owned by the shipyard of Swan, Hunter in England was christened the *Titanian*. That ship hit an iceberg off Newfoundland and was towed to shore by two rescue crafts.

Based on these cases, testing the fates seems to be ludicrous and expensive.

A Terribly Accurate Prophecy

If the following story were fiction, we would immediately dismiss it as too coincidental—almost contrived. But, as the following events were carefully documented as they occurred, we must, perhaps begrudgingly, admit that truth is often stranger than fiction.

Richard Brown had been captain of the ship *Usk* for some time. During one voyage in the early 1860s, he was relaxing in his cabin. The trip had been uneventful, and he had a very capable crew under his command. Comparatively speaking, Brown had not a care in the world. His thoughts were likely somewhat unfocused, possibly influenced by the sounds of the sea against the side of the *Usk*—sounds with which Brown was very familiar.

An instant later, though, his reverie was interrupted. There, standing 3 feet (1 meter) from him, was a woman! Brown shook his head, rubbed his eyes with his clenched fists and then dared to look again. As he did, the man's heart skipped a beat, because he knew immediately that this woman was not of flesh and blood. Her image was filmy, vaporous, not quite solid.

She beckoned to him to move closer to her. Brown reported later that he felt somehow compelled to obey this supernatural being. The man complied.

"Turn this craft around at once," she whispered to him in a weak, airy voice. "Head back for home. This ship is doomed. If you do not head back the vessel and all aboard will be lost."

With that warning the apparition disappeared as quickly as she had appeared.

Captain Richard Brown's story seems to prove that seafaring prophecies can come true.

For measurable minutes, Captain Richard Brown was unable to move. Half-formed questions flooded through his mind. *Am I losing my mind? Should I continue on our course just to spite that creature? Should I obey her ghostly warnings and turn the ship around?*

Finally, even though he would face terrible censure from the shipping line's owners and the rest of the sailing community, Brown decided to head for home. His directive took the members of the crew by surprise, but they realized that the man must be really afraid of what would happen if they were to continue on their assigned journey.

They too were well aware that by going back now, with the cargo undelivered, Captain Brown was effectively ending his career.

A few days later, when they sailed into their home port of Cardiff, Wales, the reactions that all those aboard the *Usk* had predicted began. Brown was fired and stripped of his master's ticket. From that point on, the ridicule began and never stopped. Years later, Richard Brown died, a broken and disgraced seaman.

The *Usk*, however, continued to serve her owners. As soon as another, equally well-qualified skipper was hired, the ship set out again—to complete the voyage that the ghost's visitation had foreshortened. Some weeks later, the ship's owners received a communication. The *Usk* had been spotted on the Atlantic Ocean—not far from where Brown had turned her around on the previous trip. Although the fire aboard her had almost burned itself out, some pockets of embers remained. All the crew was still on the ship when the *Usk* was boarded, but not one of them was alive.

The ghost's caution had been accurate, and Brown had been wise to obey her. Unfortunately for the new crew, the ship's owners and, of course, for Brown himself, no one realized that fact until it was too late.

Fate Fulfilled

All seafaring folk accept that seeing a ghost aboard their ship will bring bad luck to the voyage. As ghosts have many reasons for manifesting to humans, that theory cannot be correct all the time. Spirits visit the living perhaps just to say a last good-bye. Other times, a phantom will appear to warn of danger or to offer protection to those living in the earthly realm. Despite these possibilities for a haunting on board a ship, when sailors see a ghost, they are so convinced the spirit portends terrible times ahead that they act as though they are doomed.

The following incidents occurred on a brig that sailed out of Baltimore, Maryland, on March 11, 1817, heading for the West Indies. The vessel was crewed by a dozen seamen, including the captain. We know these details because the encounter was carefully documented in a book entitled *Life on the Ocean: Twenty Years at Sea*, written by George Little and published in 1843.

Mr. Little relates that the first incident occurred when the boat was just a few days into its trip, supplies were still plentiful and the men still fresh and eager. The day was as beautiful as a day at sea could possibly be—the wind was temperate, the ocean was calm and the sun was shining. Even those men without work assignments were up on deck, just enjoying the nearly perfect experience of sailing. The captain and his first mate, of course, were in the wheelhouse.

The idle chatter the crew had been exchanging slowly and naturally wound down and an atmosphere of companionable silence prevailed—until one man's screams disturbed the peace. Almost as one, the rest of the crew swung around to face the man who'd let out the terrible yell. He was frozen in place, his eyes fixed on an object toward the stern of the craft. Again, almost as one, the man's mates turned to follow the man's gaze.

There, at the stern of the ship and as clear as the day, stood the image of a woman.

None of those sailors could have thought that this vision was real. They'd done a thorough check for stowaways before leaving the harbor and they'd been at sea for days. Each man concluded, correctly as the future would disclose, that this was not a flesh-and-blood human being but the ghost of one. Their ship was haunted.

The bravest man was finally able to free his body from the paralysis of fright and ran to get the captain.

"Come quickly, sir," he urged, trying desperately to keep his voice under control. No matter what the situation, he could not have seemed to be giving an order to the ship's leader. "The men have seen a ghost, sir. She's on the deck near the stern. She's just standing there and it's frightening them half to death, I'll tell you."

"Whatever are you on about?" the older man spluttered in reply to this strange information as he got up from his captain's chair and prepared to investigate the wild claim.

When he arrived on the deck he could clearly see that his crew was in a dreadful state. What he couldn't see was what they were claiming to be staring at. Despite their best attempts to point out the ghost's image to the captain, neither he nor his first mate was able to see anything out of the ordinary.

Not long after, the ghost vanished and the men slowly resumed their chores. Those not on duty went below to their bunks and lay pondering their recent experience and the implications it would have for their immediate future.

The very next day, it seemed that the prophecy of bad luck was beginning to come true when three of the crewmen complained of being seriously ill. As a result, the remaining men had to work harder and longer to get the work done. Everyone became short-tempered and tired. The mood aboard ship deteriorated considerably.

Just when that new routine had become established on board the brig, the phantom made a second appearance on the afterdeck. This time, fewer men saw her, but again she was invisible to the captain and his first mate. The day after that second supernatural encounter, the ship sailed into a dreadful storm, proving in the minds of most of those aboard that the ghost had brought bad luck.

Before the end of the voyage had been reached, the manifestation appeared once more. Shortly after, several sailors were struck down by a mysterious fever. One of those who became ill died in his bunk.

Was the ghost there to bring tragedy to the small craft? Facts would soon prove that this was not the case at all.

As it turned out, the ghostly woman who kept appearing on deck was not actually a harbinger of evil tidings at all. She was the spirit of the captain's wife who had died a few days after her husband set sail. Presumably, she was trying in spirit to say good-bye to her beloved.

2
Supernatural
Submarine
Stories

There is something especially provocative about life on a submarine—life in the depths of the ocean where human beings should not be able to live. Add a haunting and the chill factor goes up even more.

Protected by a Dream

Scotland's most famous bridge, the Firth of Forth, is more than 100 years old, but it is still a reliable and solid piece of engineering and construction.

In Scotland, during World War I, the Countess of Chichester wrote to her friend Lord Halifax to tell him an amazing story about that bridge. It seems that the bridge survived the terrible war thanks to a dream!

Lady Chichester described visiting with her old friend Madelaine, a retired nurse. Madelaine had just that previous week experienced a very strange dream—visions of whales with castles on their backs circling around a pillar. She specifically identified this pillar as "the third pillar," even though she didn't know, at the time, exactly what that meant. When the same dream recurred the next night, she was sure it was an important message from that place beyond our immediate understanding.

Madelaine did not know the significance of the vision or who in her large circle of acquaintances needed this information. After much thought, the former nurse decided she should tell everyone she possibly could about the dream and let the people do with the information what they felt they had to.

Madelaine wrote to her nephew who worked for the company responsible for the bridge. He replied to his aunt's letter quickly, telling her "those were not whales with castles on their backs that you dreamed about. They were submarines with their periscopes up." He went on to explain that the third pillar under the Firth of Forth Bridge was the

One woman's prophetic dream appears to have spared a Scottish bridge from attack by a German U-boat.

only one that had not yet been completely reinforced against a possible attack by a German submarine.

Madelaine's nephew may have been somewhat hesitant to approach his superiors with information from an elderly relative's dream but, fortunately, he did. Those responsible for such things immediately rearranged work schedules in order to finish packing concrete around the third pillar. The day after work on the supports was completed, two German U-boats were spotted in the River Forth. Seconds later, they fired on the submerged supports but failed to do any damage because all the pillars—even the third one—had been reinforced by concrete.

The Firth of Forth Bridge was saved because of a dream experienced by a retired nurse who knew nothing about bridge construction or enemy vessels or, for that matter, even whales with castles on their backs.

Ryan's Specter

In *Lord Halifax's Ghost Book* (1936), the author relates the following supernatural submarine tale.

According to a man named Francis Cadogan who sent the information to Lord Halifax, this incident was "general knowledge among the senior submarine officers and was told by the officer commanding the Mediterranean flotilla in 1919."

It seems that during World War I, an extremely popular English naval officer, Captain Ryan, had been sent out on a mission aboard a submarine. When the vessel under his command did not return when it was expected, the authorities became alarmed and sent a search party to find the submarine. Sadly, no sign of the craft or of any of the crew was found. For a few weeks, some of Ryan's colleagues remained hopeful that the highly skilled seaman would eventually make it back to port. By the time more than a month had passed, however, everyone accepted that the ship had been lost, along with all hands on board.

Six weeks after Ryan's sub was last seen, another captain, a man named Jackson, set out in another submarine on a similar mission. At a particular point in the voyage, Captain Jackson was supposed to direct his sub to the surface and report on what he found. In preparation for this maneuver, Captain Jackson ordered that the periscope be raised.

As he peered into the periscope, Jackson was surprised and delighted to see Ryan's missing submarine on the water's surface. Better still, Ryan was standing on the bow of his ship, belted to a hatch and waving madly directly at

With the ghostly help of a missing naval officer, an English submarine captain avoided some deadly mines.

Jackson's periscope. He immediately gave orders to change course in order to rescue Ryan and any other survivors aboard the submarine that had been missing for so many weeks.

Strangely, when they reached the point where Captain Jackson had seen Captain Ryan and his ship, nothing was there to be found. Jackson was more than a bit confused since he knew for certain what he had seen. After searching the area for miles around, the disappointed submarine captain gave up and ordered his own vessel to continue on its original mission.

When Jackson and his charges returned to dock after a successful mission, they discovered that, if they had not changed their course so quickly to try to rescue Captain Ryan, they would have struck two mines. Jackson reeled with shock, for it was then that he realized the ghost of his colleague Ryan had appeared as a decoy in order to save Jackson, his submariners and his craft from certain destruction.

Eerie Explosion

The following account, reported by Raymond Lamont Brown in *Fate* magazine, June 1977, happened to the Larsen family while they were visiting Ireland in the summer of 1968.

Mr. and Mrs. Larsen and their two children were sailing down the coast of Ireland in their boat, the *Grey Seal*, enjoying the magnificent scenery when they decided to stop for dinner. The family's quiet meal aboard the deck of their sloop was disturbed by what sounded like an underwater explosion. All four Larsens were experienced sailors used to the sights and sounds of the ocean, but this was unlike anything they had ever heard before. As they stared out to the spot where the sound seemed to have come from, much to their astonishment, something began to rise up and break through the surface of the water. Impossibly, it was an old-fashioned submarine!

Mr. Larsen grabbed his binoculars to take a closer look. He could see the vessel was marked with the number 65. Then, as the four people sitting at the table on the *Grey Seal* watched, the image of the submarine became less and less distinct before vanishing from view entirely. When the family arrived back at their home port, they began to discreetly ask questions, hoping to get some answers that would help them understand their strange sighting. No helpful answers were forthcoming, unfortunately.

Mr. Larsen's curiosity would not let him rest until he obtained at least some insight into what he and his family had seen that summer afternoon. He visited the library at a nearby university where he found a book about submarine action during World War I. He read that on July 10, 1918, an American submarine had torpedoed a German U-boat at exactly the coordinates where he had anchored the *Grey Seal* that beautiful summer afternoon just a few weeks prior. Seconds later, a further coincidence came to Larsen's mind—his family's visit had been exactly 50 years to the day after that wartime event.

Now Larsen was really intrigued and knew he needed to find out as many of the details of that incident as still existed. Soon he learned that what had actually happened was that an American lieutenant named Foster had been directing his submarine—the AL2—toward an enemy submarine. There was an underwater explosion unconnected with Foster's ship, and the German sub disintegrated before the American submarine had come near it. That U-boat was designated UB-65.

Intrigued by what his investigation had thus far revealed, Larsen wondered if he and his family had somehow witnessed a retrocognitive incident—that is, had observed a psychic reenactment of the wartime explosion. Further checking revealed that UB-65 had been thought of as a jinxed craft from the moment she was put out to sea.

At her launch, the sub had come free of her moorings and crushed a worker. When her hull was being tested for air tightness, the engine room somehow filled with gas and three men were asphyxiated. On her first submersion, she became stuck on the seafloor. By the time the submarine was freed, more of her crew was dead than alive. Her captain ordered that they follow a certain course to join the rest of the submarine fleet in the area. As they made their way toward the supposed safety in numbers, a torpedo aboard the UB-65 exploded, killing yet another man.

If there could be anything more intimidating than serving in a submarine, it would have to be serving in a haunted submarine, and that is exactly what the UB-65 became. From that day on, the spirit of the man killed by the torpedo wandered the hallways. Despite the obvious jinx on this ship, she continued to serve. More men were killed and those who weren't killed lived in abject fear, for they knew that a haunted ship was an evil ship.

The moment the sub docked, the crew fled. As they looked back, they could see their fellow sailor's ghost, standing on top of the U-boat, staring pointedly at them. None of those who'd been on that mission ever boarded the UB-65 again. Surprisingly, the authorities had the ship blessed and then assigned a new, handpicked, crew to her. These men were chosen partly because they knew nothing of the horrendously bad luck the vessel had experienced so far.

The German sub set out again. Within hours, one of the men had killed himself and another had broken a leg and then developed a raging fever. By nightfall the next day, yet another sailor had killed himself. The very next day, they were downed by underwater enemy fire. Using incredible skill, the captain of the seemingly cursed UB-65 managed to raise his charge from the bottom of the ocean, but every man on board reported seeing "ghostly figures" and a "greenish-white light" throughout the craft. Like the crew before them, this group of submariners also fled the ship the moment it docked.

Economics dictated that the Germans could not merely set this hoodoo craft aside and use another one in her place. The sub was repaired and yet another crew was found and she sailed again.

After the UB-65 set out this time, she was never seen again. A German psychologist released the following statement: "This phenomenon does not lend itself to an explanation. I can put forward no alternative theory to the supernatural agency [the ghostly figures] that finally brought about the destruction of the ill-fated vessel. There is no evidence of any kind of plot and the facts do not fit with any known type of mass hallucination."

So, in the end, all of Larsen's detailed searching was rewarded, for he was by then completely convinced that, off the Irish coast in 1968, he and his family had seen a phantom ship. Not only had they seen the ghost of the jinxed German U-boat—UB-65, but they also heard the sounds of her destruction.

3
Haunted
Lighthouses

Lighthouses are unique, unusual and an extremely important part of the seafaring world. For hundreds of years they have been beacons for sailors as well as romantic images for those on the land. Although the towers are now being automated, until recently lighthouses also provided isolated homes to unique, unusual and extremely important people who operated the warning beacons. It is not surprising that so many of these installations are haunted.

Haunted Rock

The waves of the Atlantic Ocean lap against Great Issacs Rock, which stands 55 miles (88 kilometers) due east of Fort Lauderdale, Florida, near the Bahama Islands. This rock is enormous, nearly a mile in length. As it was a serious potential threat to navigation, it badly needed a warning beacon constructed on it.

Oddly, the building chosen to be the lighthouse on Great Issacs Rock was not designed to serve that purpose. This engineering marvel was intended as a showpiece for the 1851 Great Exposition held in London, England. The tower was 152 feet (46 meters) tall and was built solely of iron. During the Exposition, the structure attracted even more attention than the builders had hoped, so the owners left it assembled and in place for several years.

When the tower was finally dismantled, the job was done carefully and according to the builder's instructions. This meant it could be rebuilt anywhere at any time with a minimum of trouble. At some point shortly after it had been disassembled, someone with great vision realized that the tower, which was now without a purpose, could be shipped to Great Issacs Rock and reassembled as a much needed lighthouse.

It took three large sailing vessels to carry the parts of the tower from England to its new home on the Rock. Workers who had taken the structure apart in London were also aboard those ships so they could reassemble the monolith on its new rocky home. Once there, however, many of those construction workers did not want to stay

The ghost of Great Isaac's Rock is known as the Gray Lady.

to finish their assignment. They were too frightened. They had seen the Rock's ghost, the "Gray Lady."

Legend has it that the story behind this haunting is sorrowful. Apparently many years before, during a severe storm, a ship crashed against the Rock, killing all aboard except an infant. Rescuers, who had been sent out from the nearest port, found the child alive and virtually unharmed. These Good Samaritans cared for the baby until its family in England could be found and they made arrangements for the child to be transported to them.

It became common knowledge among those who sailed near the Great Issacs Rock that the baby's mother appeared regularly on the jagged outcropping. Just before every full moon, sailors said they could see her form walking the length of the rock and hear her cries as she mourned her own death and the loss of her beloved baby.

Unfortunately for those frightened construction workers, no matter how much they wanted to get off the rock, there was no way they could. None of the three ships had stayed to wait for them. As a result, the workers were stranded on an uninhabitable, haunted and completely isolated island.

In order to get off this horrible place as quickly as possible, the workers did everything they could to speed the rebuilding process. And, a few weeks later, leaving the important legacy of a lighthouse behind them, the men gratefully boarded the ship that had come to take them back to England.

At least now the dangerous area of the Great Issacs Rock was marked and, hopefully, there would never be another accident such as the one that caused the outcropping to become haunted in the first place.

For many years, the hastily assembled lighthouse did its job warning ships of the rock's existence, but the island apparently remained haunted. Lighthouse keepers maintained that they could see a woman's ghostly image and hear her mournful moans as she continued to walk the length and breadth of the giant rock roughly once a month—just before a full moon.

One of those keepers decided that he should have the island blessed in the hopes that the ghost's sad soul would finally move on to the great beyond. Some say the exorcism was a success. Others say that it is not so, that the cleansing ritual did not free the ghost from her terrible visits.

All of this might not matter too much by now except for an incident on August 4, 1969, when Mr. B. Millings and Mr. Ivan Major disappeared. The two had been posted to the Great Issacs Light sometime before and had proven themselves to be reliable workers. To this day, no one has ever seen either Millings or Major alive, nor does anyone know for certain what happened to them. According to Fred Stonehouse, author of *Ghost Ships*, the men "simply vanished."

It's too late now for us to find out what happened to the men or whether their disappearance had anything to do with the ghost. Speculation was once rampant and even included rumors about UFOs being in the area at that time. When all of that scuttlebutt settled, only the facts remained—two men vanished from a haunted island in the Atlantic Ocean.

Even today, speculation about this ghost story could still lead us to any conclusion.

Gentle Rue

It would be difficult to picture a more idyllic lighthouse than the one at Heceta Head, north of Florence, Oregon, and just north of the famous Sea Lion Caves. The mist-enshrouded coastline gives the lighthouse, its auxiliary buildings and the promontory on which they stand a softened look. It is perhaps most suitable that the ghost haunting this lighthouse is a benign and gentle soul. Sadly, however, if general belief and deductive reasoning are accurate, the spirit is a woman filled with grief.

History tells us that in the 1890s, when the light at Heceta Head was first installed, one of the men charged with operating the machinery was married and had a newborn daughter. Historical records also indicate that this keeper did not stay on the job for long. Legend has it that the baby died. Her body is apparently buried somewhere on the lighthouse property. The ghost who haunts the grounds is presumed to be the infant's mother.

For the most part, her ghostly presence resides in the assistant lightkeeper's residence. The haunting never upsets anyone because she is such a gentle entity. When Carol and Mike Korgan moved onto the property, they were curious about the identity of this ghost that they already suspected was female. They purchased a Ouija board and asked the spirit to identify herself. The board's planchette spelled out the name "Rue" and the Korgans have called the ghost by that name ever since.

She has been credited with moving small objects around. Rue becomes most active when work is being done on the house that she would have lived in when she

A ghost named Rue haunts Heceta Head Lighthouse near Florence, Oregon.

was alive. Rue is not a trouble-maker but she *is* a stickler for detail.

She seemed to be displeased, for instance, with some interior decorating that a group of volunteers was doing at the lighthouse. The volunteer painters stayed the night in the residence in order not to waste valuable time commuting to and from their task. Throughout the night the fire alarm sounded every few hours for no apparent reason. The workers, who were trying to sleep, eventually took the battery out of the alarm so they would not be disturbed. Unfortunately for them, the fire alarm continued to sound occasionally over the remainder of the night even though it no longer had a power source.

By the summer of 1963, the lighthouse at Heceta Head was automated and the residences abandoned. By 1970, the haunted house and all the other buildings on the property had fallen into a dangerous condition and there was talk of demolishing them. Some citizens with an eye to preservation stepped in, and Rue's house, along with the other buildings, was saved from the wrecker's ball.

Major repair work was needed, and Rue seemed to be disturbed when repairs began on "her" home. One day, as a carpenter worked inside the house, he was most surprised to see a woman's reflection in one of the windows. He swung around and saw that he was no longer alone in the room. A woman had clearly joined him—a woman with silver-gray hair and old-fashioned clothing. He stared mutely at the apparition, who stared right back at him with eyes that seemed to plead for help. Knowing full well that he had just come face to face with Rue and that she was not of this earth, the man did not linger at his post long enough to determine what it was she was pleading for him to do.

The worker refused to ever enter the house again, even after he accidentally broke a window in the place. He replaced the pane from the outside and left the job of sweeping up the debris to someone else. Later that day, workers heard scratching sounds coming from the floor of the room where the window had been broken. The next day when they went into the room, they found the glass shards swept neatly into a pile even though no one—well, at least no one living—had been in there.

Since then, the houses and all the buildings at Heceta Head have been restored to represent different eras of the lighthouse. Some replicate the original 1890s look while others are representative of the 1930s. Almost all the buildings around the lighthouse are utilized for some purpose or another.

Many visitors to the site report hearing lady-like footsteps coming from vacant rooms and catching a glimpse of an elderly woman's face staring down at them from a window in a particular room. Some folks have even spoken of seeing the ghost in that same room. Everyone who has seen her is immediately aware that the person they are looking at is not a flesh-and-blood being. Rather she appears to be made of a smoky mist or vapor.

If Rue wants company in her afterlife she doesn't have far to go, for the ghost of a man who has been named John arrived at Heceta Head in 1996. The Korgans believe that his energy came to the property on, or in, a couch that they moved from a house they had previously owned.

Mike Korgan is apparently especially fond of John. He credits the ghost with being a very comforting presence and one who is certainly as welcome as Rue's ghost in their unique home, where they now operate a very successful bed and breakfast. If you have the chance, drop in and enjoy one of the Korgan's internationally famous breakfasts. You might also enjoy watching the History Channel video or reading the article in *Life* magazine, both devoted to the haunted lighthouse at Heceta Head.

If you have a chance to encounter these ghosts, please do offer your kind regards to Rue and John!

Yesterday's News

Fort (or Fortress) Monroe, on Chesapeake Bay in Virginia, is one of the oldest active military installations in the United States. Not surprisingly, then, there are those who say many of the buildings are, by now, haunted. But a ghost story involving the fort's lighthouse, the oldest building on the grounds, was already making international headlines in 1867.

The *Gleaner*, Chatham, New Brunswick's newspaper, for instance, ran the story in full, even though the text took up more than 4 feet (1.2 meters) of column space (roughly 1200 words) in the edition printed on June 29, 1867. Under the headline "THE GHOST IN THE LIGHT-HOUSE," an unnamed reporter began by explaining that this haunted lighthouse on Cape Charles was a Union holding during the Civil War and, to this day, a "great bulwark" or breakwater between "the tide waters of Virginia and Maryland."

He went on to describe the tower, built in 1802, which remains standing today, as "a very plain tower; some 60 feet [18 meters] in height, with an ordinary, old-fashioned lantern…Looking at it, you would never think it [could have been] the scene of a regular ghost story, which was, for the time, about as dreadful and mysterious as anything could be."

During the 1850s, the light was managed by a widow named Mrs. Lane and her teenaged son, Dick. One night in March 1856, a terrible windstorm blew up. The gales were so strong that Mrs. Lane could barely stand still against them, let alone walk outside. Unfortunately, it was

Several ghosts haunt the lighthouse and neighboring quarters at Fort Monroe on Virginia's Chesapeake Bay.

on that very night that a guard from the fort came and knocked on her door. He could not have had worse news for the woman. The beacon light in the tower had somehow gone out. Ships at sea were in peril without the benefit of this vital navigational aid.

Mrs. Lane had no hope of repairing the problem on her own. Fortunately, the kindly soldier offered to help her in any way that he could. After wrapping herself in a shawl and hood, the woman joined the man outside, and together they battled the winds while collecting the materials they thought they'd need to restore the light beam.

Grateful to be protected from the wind once again, the two stepped inside the tower building. They stood still and quiet for a moment while their eyes adjusted to the darkness and their ears to the more muffled wind sounds.

Just as they were about to head up the stairs to the light room, a new sound made them pause. "The sound came heavy and dull from the top of the tower, like someone slowly and heavily descending the steps. Tramp, tramp, tramp!"

The widow Lane cried out, "Mercy on me!…Someone is in the lantern."

The soldier shouted, "Who are you and what are you doing there?"

The report continued, "There was a pause in the sound; and then a wild, hollow voice rang through the tower. 'Woe, woe to the ships! Woe to the ships!'

"The soldier and the widow wanted to hear no more, but, in another moment found themselves [outside] at the foot of the tower. In a few minutes, a dark figure issued from the doorway and moved slowly down the beach, until it disappeared in the darkness."

Additional soldiers were called from the fort and a thorough search of the lighthouse was undertaken. They didn't find anyone hiding in the tower, but they did discover that extinguishers had been placed over the beacon lamps.

The article went on to explain, "Extinguishing the lamps in a lighthouse, without proper authority, is a criminal offence, and a reward was immediately offered for the perpetrator of this crime. The next night the commandant of the fort stationed a sentinel near the tower, to watch if anyone should attempt to enter it, and arrest or fire upon whatever should do so.

"It was a dark night and the wind was howling across the bay and along the [nearby Hampton Roads]. Towards 10 o'clock, a fierce shrill blast struck the Point and dashed a quantity of sand into the sentinel's eyes, completely blinding him for the time. When he recovered the use of them again he glanced at the tower and to his dismay, found that it was in total darkness. He had been unable to see for the space of five minutes; but previous to that, he was sure no one had entered the lighthouse.

"He hurried to the tower and entering it sprang up the stairs, gun in hand. He paused. The footfalls the widow had described were heard again. In a moment, however, a tall figure was seen descending the stairs. [The soldier] sprang towards [the image] but a powerful hand dashed him aside and a wild voice rang through the tower, 'Woe, woe to the ships!'

"Still undismayed, the soldier hurried down the steps; and when he reached the beach…he saw a figure disappearing in the darkness. Instantly he raised his gun and fired. The report of the sentinel's musket brought [another] guard, this one with torches and lanterns."

Together, the two soldiers, more frightened than they cared to admit, searched the area, but could not find anyone or anything out of the ordinary.

Before long, word of this phantom intruder had spread throughout the fort and neighboring community.

"It was the strangest affair that ever happened at Old Point; and the superstition and curiosity of the inhabitants of the little peninsula were excited to the highest pitch."

Of all those involved in the eerie event, though, Dick Lane was definitely the most upset. He asked for permission to guard the light alone the next night armed with a pistol. "The permission was granted but the commandant gave orders to have a guard of five kept in readiness, just outside of the fort, to proceed to Dick's assistance as soon as they should hear the report of the pistol.

"The night was as wild as either of the others, but Dick took his post in the lantern, undismayed, and prepared to await the coming of the ghost. About 10 o'clock, he began to be sleepy, but was at length aroused from this state by the sound of heavy footsteps on the stairs. He listened. The sound came near. Then he heard a wild mournful voice crying, 'Woe, woe to the ships!'

"The lad felt his blood run cold; but summoned up his courage [and] prepared himself for the encounter." He turned quickly around and came face to face with a ghastly vision, "[a] tall muscular figure, clad in a faded blue uniform, with a haggard face overgrown with beard, and with long matted hair."

Before Dick had a chance to gather his wits about him, the specter "glared at him savagely, and then sprang towards him with a howl of rage. Dick raised his pistol and fired but missed his aim. In another instant the figure seized him by the throat. The boy struggled manfully; but he was no match for the powers of his strange antagonist. [Dick] was forced to the floor; and the grip about his throat tightened, until he grew unconscious.

"When [Dick] recovered his senses he was lying on the beach [near the tower] and the commandant of the fort was throwing water in his face. Springing to his feet, he asked hurriedly, 'Are the lights burning?' "

After the commandant assured the worried young man that all was well with the beam from the lighthouse, the older man went on to explain that the sound of the gun-shot had signaled the guards that there was trouble. "They arrived just in time to save him from death at the hand of the ghost."

The lengthy article concluded by stating only one side of the dramatic events—that the ghost was not, in fact, a ghost at all but rather a deranged soldier who had escaped from the Fort's hospital and, once recaptured, was sent to a "lunatic asylum." Not everyone who heard that rendi-tion of the tale believed it. Many believed that a ghost had been stalking about the lighthouse at Fort Monroe. If you wish to determine which of the two theories you think is correct, you can visit the beacon. The oldest structure on the base is still an operating navigational aid, although it was automated in 1973 and no one—in this life or the next—is responsible for keeping the beam shining.

If, after your inspection, you think that the phantom visitor was a flesh-and-blood intruder, then please don't think your visit has been wasted, for there are other con-firmed hauntings at Fort Monroe.

The Woman in White is the ghost of an unfaithful wife. She had been married to a military captain who murdered her when he found out about her infidelities. Her spirit is said to haunt a part of the Fort often referred to as Ghost Alley. You can also find another ghost—this one with a strange aversion. She too, haunts a home on Ghost Alley. It doesn't take long for anyone assigned to live in that particular residence (and these residences are still occupied by military personnel and their families) to discover that bringing roses into their home is a shameful waste. The rose petals will inevitably be found strewn all over the floor the next day.

In a neighboring house, children's laughter can be heard even though no reasonable explanation for such noise can be provided. In addition, if any living children are residing in the house, some of their toys will disappear for a time, only to show up again days later. No corporeal reason for these annoyances has ever been discovered.

Legend has it that the ghosts of both General Ulysses S. Grant and President Abe Lincoln have been seen nearby in a room at Fort Monroe's Officers' Quarters. Their images are reported to be sitting at a desk, looking very troubled.

The spirit of Jefferson Davis, president of the Confederacy during the Civil War, haunts the prison building, no doubt because he was imprisoned there for a period just before the end of the war.

Perhaps the strangest haunting anywhere near this lighthouse comes from the ghost of Edgar Allen Poe. When Poe was a young soldier stationed at Fort Monroe, he wrote his well-regarded short story "The Cask of Amontillado."

And so, Fort (or Fortress) Monroe, on Chesapeake Bay in Virginia, is still an active place—on at least two separate planes of existence.

Lingering Lass

Although Hilton Head Island is in South Carolina, it is geographically closer to Savannah, Georgia, than to any other major city. It is also worth noting that the island stands exposed to some of the most treacherous weather known.

Legend has it that at one time the Hilton Head Lighthouse keeper was a widowed man responsible for looking after his 16-year-old daughter. He was a hard worker who made sure that no detail was ever overlooked. The light's wicks were always trimmed and oiled with great care, the glass surrounding the light always polished to a high gleam. Because of this care, the keeper had won awards of recognition from his superiors for his work.

After supper every evening, the man would climb the circular staircase to double check the light and to make sure that everything would be well until morning. He kept to this routine every night—in fair weather or foul. This was why, when he left the residence to begin his rounds during a bad storm, his daughter thought nothing of it.

In the few minutes it took him to reach the top of the lighthouse, the storm had strengthened into a hurricane. Wind and sleeting rain pelted against the glass protecting the light. As experienced a keeper as he was, the man had never seen such a vicious storm. It was as if the seas and winds had been stirred by the devil himself.

The man's heart was torn. Should he stay and do what he could to keep the light shining, or should he go back downstairs and care for his daughter who must have become terrified? Finally, he decided that he could do

*Traumatized by her father's death inside Hilton Head Lighthouse,
a little girl continues to haunt the property.*

both and that he would leave his post for a few minutes to check on the child.

Meanwhile, in the living quarters, the girl too was wondering what she should do. Should she stay where she was relatively safe or should she go to help her father? She soon decided that she would at least have to assure herself that her father was all right before she could relax at all. So she dressed as best she could to protect herself against the weather and went out in search of the older man.

Minutes later, the girl found her father. He was unconscious, near the bottom step of the lighthouse. The child panicked. What could she possibly do? How could she help her father? How could she keep the light that was so badly needed by mariners lit? Would help arrive in time to prevent a tragedy?

Sadly, the answer to that last question proved to be "no." It was fully a week before the time the weather had calmed sufficiently for anyone to get to the stranded light-house keeper and his daughter. By that time, the man had died from the effects of the heart attack he had suffered while at the bottom of the concrete steps. His beloved daughter had also died. Her lifeless body was found lying beside his. No one was ever able to determine a reason for her death. Most people who knew the pair guessed that she had died from grief.

Although the man's soul seems to have gone on to its final reward, the girl's spirit has haunted the property for decades. She is seen dressed in the clothes she was wearing when would-be rescuers found her earthly remains. The pretty young ghost makes herself visible whenever a storm approaches. Her transparent image runs toward people as they come toward the tower. She waves her arms at them, signaling that they should not come any closer. Then she vanishes.

One couple maintain that they picked up a teenaged girl at the side of a road near the lighthouse during a severe rainstorm. The child gratefully climbed into the back seat of the couple's car. As the man began to drive away, his wife turned to ask the poor drenched girl where they could take her. No one was in their back seat, even though both the man and the woman knew for certain that they had just let a very wet youngster into the warmth and security of their car. They were so shocked that they pulled over to the side of the road again immediately. The man climbed into the back seat to look for the girl. She was nowhere to be found, but one section of the back seat was inexplicably wet.

The poor child's spirit seems to have been so horror-struck by the terrible tragedy that it cannot rest. Hopefully her torment has, at least, protected others ever since the haunting began.

Basement Bogey

In the spring of 1993, Jerry and Jeff were two members of a Coast Guard delegation assigned to repaint and restore the fire-damaged lighthouse at Standard Rock, on a shoal in Lake Superior near Duluth, Minnesota.

Jeff began his recounting of that experience by explaining why the work needed to be done. It seems that the lighthouse and related property was to be turned over to the National Park Service but extensive repairs had to be made first. The building had been abandoned since 1961 when a fatal fire had all but destroyed it.

Jeff explained, "The job ahead of us was big, but simple. We had to fix what needed to be fixed, then clean and paint. Each of us had a task to do."

Such a calm, matter-of-fact description seemed to indicate anticipation of an uneventful assignment. Unfortunately, that was not to be the case. Even the trip to the shoal was a strange one.

Jeff recalled that the sail to a point near the shoal was uneventful. That smooth sailing, however, was about to

Two members of the Coast Guard were terrified by forces unknown as they renovated a lighthouse near Duluth, Minnesota.

change. "As soon as we arrived near the lighthouse, the weather began to deteriorate. Eventually, it began to blow so hard that we had to drop the anchor and ride it out. After two days of this, the weather calmed sufficiently for us to take the work party ashore in a small boat."

Once the group had landed, they lost no time in starting the job. A few hours later, "the weather started to turn bad again." For this reason, the workers decided to stay at the tasks as long as they possibly could and to spend the night at the lighthouse.

At one point early that evening, Jerry and his friend Jeff took a break from their chores at the same time. The two began talking about the fire that had gutted the lighthouse and killed three lighthouse keepers. Perhaps to ward off the possibility of such talk becoming too serious, Jerry decided to joke around a bit. He opened the door to the stairway leading to a lower level. He knew that none of the members of the clean-up committee were down there and that he was talking to nothingness, but nevertheless he hollered into the cold, damp, dark stairway, "Hey, we're going to have a bite to eat. Want anything?"

Jerry's attempt at humor to defuse the situation had the opposite effect. "Immediately, we heard sounds from the level below. There was scraping and knocking, but the most chilling were the sounds of footsteps coming up the stairs. Jeff and I looked at each other. His eyes were as large as Volkswagen head lights and I bet mine were just as big. Not saying a word, we both raced up the stairs to the main level."

Despite their fear, they did get something to eat and the food helped calm their recently shattered nerves so much that they decided they "had imagined the whole thing." As a matter of fact, just to prove that it had all been silliness, "Jeff related the story to the rest of the crew and everyone had a good laugh."

At that point, work resumed until just after 11 PM, when "a couple of the guys suggested going down to the basement at midnight just to see if anything would happen."

Jeff had to admit that he wasn't really keen on the idea but, at the same time, he didn't want "to be branded a coward." So, at the stroke of midnight, "five of us made our way to the basement." They called out a greeting to whatever might have been there and then set about waiting in the dark basement of the abandoned lighthouse. For a few minutes, there was only silence. Then Jeff knew that he was feeling something.

"The hair was standing up on the back of my neck. I swear I could feel something moving around us. I'm sure that I was not the only one either."

After a few moments of experiencing this eerie sensation, they decided to go back upstairs to the keepers' quarters. "As soon as we were all out of the basement, the sounds started again. For a minute or so, the five of us just stared at each other. Then we heard footsteps coming up the stairs. We all tried to get away at the same time. It was total chaos. As luck would have it, I was the last in line. As I was going up the stairs, I glanced back and, just for an instant, saw a shadow with no definite shape to it emerge from the basement door."

Now this was a group of people specifically chosen and trained to be brave and strong at all times, so they knew how to react to a paranormal encounter. They all went straight to denial. Without so much as saying a word to one another, they clearly decided to ignore the fact that something pretty strange had just occurred.

"We just went back to work. When we finished working, it was about 3 AM and we moved to the upper level of the lighthouse and tried to get some sleep. It wasn't easy, though, because for the rest of the night we heard everything from banging on the walls to distant moans. When the sun finally came up and we went back downstairs, we found that our gear had been scattered around."

In addition, "a garbage can had been turned on its side

and it looked like somebody, or something, had jumped up and down on it."

Hardcore Coast Guard members or not, Jerry, Jeff and their colleagues had finished what they'd come to the lighthouse to do and they lost no time in departing from the shoal. As they made their way in the small boat toward the ship that had brought them to Standard Rock, they wondered what had caused all of the strange activity— even the sudden storm that had almost prevented them from landing and doing their work.

Jerry closed by admitting, "I've never known what caused this, but I'm certain that, whatever it was, it wasn't of this earth."

Phantom Warning

Georgetown, in South Carolina, is one of the busiest ports on the Atlantic seaboard. Since 1801, a tall and proud lighthouse on North Island, near Georgetown, has guarded the spot where the waters of Winyah Bay have mixed with those of the Atlantic Ocean. As there were no other buildings on the island, the lighthouse keepers were among the most secluded in what was already a very isolated line of work.

For many years, the North Island light was operated by a keeper and his young daughter. They made the trip to Georgetown for supplies and entertainment, as frequently as possible but, as their only form of transportation was a rowboat, it was not a voyage they undertook on a whim. The trip could be treacherous. Journeys to the mainland had to be carefully timed so that the man would be on the island, and therefore on the job, when he was needed and so that they weren't in the water when it was too choppy.

For years, all had gone well with the father and daughter. He was able to do his work while making sure that his daughter had the material possessions she needed and some exposure to other people. One afternoon, after a most enjoyable visit to the shops on the mainland, they were returning to the lighthouse when a storm suddenly hit. Within minutes, rain was pelting down on the tiny craft and the two people in it. The little girl bailed water out of the rowboat as fast as she could, but she was not able to keep up with the rain and waves pouring into the boat. Her father pulled as hard as he could on the oars but the huge waves heaved the boat up and down and he was unable to make much headway.

The waves became bigger and bigger. One swept right across the flimsy rowboat and tossed the child overboard and into the angry sea. The terrified man immediately jumped into the water after his daughter but was not able to reach the child. He tried and tried until, just as she was sinking under the surface, he was able to grab hold of a piece of her clothing.

After fighting the gale-force winds and the angry sea, he had no energy left to lift either himself or his daughter into the rowboat. The best he could do was to cling to the side of his tiny craft. This was the pitiful sight that greeted the crew of a fishing vessel when they sailed near the small boat.

The fishermen performed an amazing rescue and, just before he lost consciousness, the man managed to express his thanks to his rescuers.

"Thank you for saving my daughter and me," the man said before passing out. He slept for hours but as soon as he woke up he wanted to see his child.

"You mentioned your daughter when we picked you up but you were alone. We figured you were just hallucinating."

"No, no!" the father screamed. "My daughter, she was with me. I must find her."

Not surprisingly, no one ever found the man's beloved daughter. His rescuers delivered him safely to his North Island home and, it is said, he never left there again. Locals brought him any supplies he needed and, years later, he died alone at the lighthouse.

Sailors still report seeing the pathetic image of a man and a little girl in a rowboat, battling the waves as they are tossed about when a storm hits. By now, such a sighting is taken as a phantom warning to all to get off the water immediately since the storm that is building will be a killer.

Ghosts Old and New

Not many buildings in North America have been standing since 1871. Of those that have, very few are referred to as "new." The New Presque Isle Lighthouse, on Lake Huron's shores near Alpena, Michigan, is an intriguing exception. Standing at a height of more than 110 feet, the tower is a tall and proud sentinel. It is also said to be the home of a ghost.

No hard facts remain to support the claim that the tower is haunted but even so, the legend has never died. The story behind that legend tells us that in the 1880s, Mr. and Mrs. Patrick Garrity were appointed to serve at the New Presque Isle Lighthouse. During their tenure, Mrs. Garrity apparently became quite demented. Some say it was the loneliness and the isolation that disturbed the woman's mental facilities. Others say it was her husband's cruelty that pushed her over the emotional edge. Whichever version might be the truth, there is little doubt that the poor woman suffered terribly during her last years at the lighthouse.

In order to keep this terrible situation a secret, Patrick Garrity, it is said, used to keep his wife locked in the basement of the tower. She was hidden from sight, but still her cries could be heard by anyone near the property.

Eventually, the pathetic, demented woman died—some say Garrity murdered his wife, others say she died of natural causes. By now we can never know for certain, just as we don't know where her earthly remains lie because, to his dying day, Patrick Garrity refused to say. She might be buried under a patch of land near the lighthouse, or her body might be encased in the place where he had hidden her for all those years. Her whereabouts are a mystery. All we know for sure is that she remains hidden to this day.

Mrs. Garrity's body may not be easy to find but her spirit apparently is, for many say that her ghostly cries of misery and injustice can be heard echoing throughout the New Presque Isle Lighthouse. Others feel the cries are not so loud and piercing as that. One woman, Anna Hoge, a lighthouse keeper's daughter, described the sound as being more like a "cat meowing or purring." Some, like Anna's father, who've heard those more sub-dued cries, think that the sounds are actually the tower itself weeping.

Although that tale cannot be documented, it is such a classic haunted lighthouse story that it couldn't have been excluded from this book!

☠

So, if the "new" lighthouse at Presque Isle can be haunted then it's only reasonable that the "old" one should be too. And it is!

The Old Presque Isle Lighthouse was built in 1840 by an experienced contractor named Jeremiah Moors. The tower is a mere 30 feet (9 meters) tall and could just barely be seen from the lake. This, of course, meant that it was virtually useless as a warning beacon. Understandably, during the 30 years it was operational, local sailors came to refer to the lighthouse as "the mistake on the lake."

After the necessary resources were found to build a replacement lighthouse, the old one was decommissioned.

The diminutive tower stood empty for 30 years before a family purchased it to live in. For 50 years members of that one family lived in the unique—and unhaunted property. After that no one lived in the Old Presque Isle Lighthouse until 1977, when George and Lorraine Parris bought the place to be their summer home. The couple thoroughly enjoyed living there. Lorraine once told a visitor that it was like "heaven" to her and that she "loved" being at the old lighthouse facility.

Over the years the Parrises opened their historic property to tourists. George would show groups of people around the place. He talked about the history of the light and showed them naval artifacts that he had collected. Lorraine was in charge of the museum part of the operation and both husband and wife enjoyed their "jobs" tremendously. Then, in the evening after the last tourist had left the place, the two would sit and have a quiet few hours together. Occasionally, during such companionable evenings, George would enjoy a glass of whisky.

This happy routine continued until 1992 when George suddenly died of a heart attack. Lorraine's world was shaken to its core. Her best friend and partner was gone. At first she didn't want to stay at the lighthouse but eventually she decided that it was her home and that she really didn't want to leave it. Within months of George's death it had become clear that he couldn't leave it either.

After a day away from home, Lorraine was driving back toward the lighthouse. As she approached the grounds she was shocked to see that there seemed to be a light shining from the tower. This, she thought, was impossible as there was no power to the light nor any bulb in the fixture. By the time she reached home all was in darkness as it should have been. After all, once such a navigational signal has been decommissioned it is illegal for the light to be turned on.

By the next morning, Lorraine was convinced that she had only imagined seeing the light, but just to make sure she climbed the stairs to the area surrounding the old lamp. Everything was as it should have been. No electrical cords or cables were anywhere to be seen and the light socket was empty. Lorraine decided not to say anything to anybody about the glow she'd thought she'd seen the night before. Perhaps she'd just been tired.

Other people, however, must have also seen the strange glow from the retired beacon, because word of the strange phenomenon spread. For miles around, people began coming to see the phantom light in operation. Soon Lorraine found members of the Coast Guard at her door requesting that she extinguish the beam. She informed the uniformed officers that she "would be glad to turn it off if they could tell her how…"

Likely rather surprised by the candid reply, the Coast Guard representatives climbed the tower to see whether something was wrong with the old lamp. They left dissatisfied, with only an official description of it being an "unidentified" light.

And even though no skeptic can explain why, the Old Presque Isle beacon still glows from "dusk to daylight" seven days of every week in every year. The gleam has actually been credited with guiding many boaters safely to shore.

Lorraine and other believers in spirits are convinced that George's ghost is manning the light. His manifestation might have been the reason a child touring the lighthouse refused to go up the tower's last few stairs. No one else in the party could see anything, but the little girl was certain that there was a man standing at the top of the stairs. She even explained what the image that she had seen looked like. She accurately described the recently deceased George Parris. And, she would have had no way of knowing that part of George's routine when he was conducting tours was to stand at the entrance to the lantern room.

Lorraine herself has experienced more personal encounters with her late husband. During a terrible thunderstorm over the September long weekend in 1992, Lorraine was ready to leave the house for a pre-planned outing. When she tried to get out the door she discovered her "round white metal table and two chairs" were jammed in front of the doorway. She tried to move the furniture out of her way but found that she couldn't budge it. Seconds later a tremendous bolt of lightning hit the path she would have been standing on if she had gone out. To this day she's grateful to George's ghost for preventing her from taking that potentially deadly step.

Some mornings Lorraine has also smelled George's favorite breakfast cooking when she first walks into the kitchen. And one evening when some old friends of George's gathered in the lantern room they poured a glass of whisky for their friend beyond. The next morning Lorraine could smell the whisky but no one has ever been able to find the glass that it had been poured into.

Children on the old lighthouse grounds will periodically ask about the man waving to them from the tower. As George loved children it's not hard to guess who or what they might be looking at.

And so, in effect, George and Lorraine Parris have continued to live in and run the Old Presque Isle Lighthouse together—even more than a decade after George's death.

Happily, both lighthouses, Old and New, are open both to the public and to discussing the ghostly legends that surround the lighthouses on Lake Huron near Alpena, Michigan.

A Veritable Gaggle of Ghosts

Authorities at some haunted venues deny that there is any truth to rumors that ghosts haunt their properties. Those representing other haunted places embrace and celebrate the fact that they are haunted. Fortunately for our purposes here, the folks responsible for the St. Augustine Lighthouse on Anastasia Island near Fort Lauderdale, Florida, stand firmly in the latter category. They even host ghost tours!

This lighthouse has had plenty of opportunity to become haunted since its construction in 1874. William Harn, the first lighthouse keeper at the St. Augustine beacon, died on the job—suddenly and from unknown causes. His earthly remains are buried at the beacon's base. It is thought, though, that Harn's spirit has not rested peacefully at the lighthouse he cared for and that his ghost is one of those that haunt the property.

Many eyewitnesses have described paranormal encounters at the St. Augustine Lighthouse on Anastasia Island, Florida.

Harn's restless soul may be the reason people feel frightened in the basement of the tower. Just a few years ago, lighthouse historian Kathy Fleming told a film crew about her experience when she had to go down to the cold, dark basement alone. At first, nothing seemed out of the ordinary but then, for reasons she didn't understand, Kathy began to feel afraid. She tried to talk herself out of the feeling, but when she realized that there was a light on in a rarely used corner closet of the lower level, the hairs on her arms began to stand straight up.

As she tried to open the door to turn off the light, she heard a nearby noise. It didn't sound like any noise she'd ever heard before. She turned toward the sound and found herself face to face with the misty figure of a tall, thin man. He was dressed in a uniform that Kathy immediately recognized as one of those worn by lighthouse keepers years ago.

For a second, Kathy stared at the manifestation that she knew had to be the ghost of a man. She could clearly make out his facial features, especially his sunken eyes. Slowly she came to realize that the strange sound she'd been hearing was the sound of the ghost breathing. Seconds later, the vision and the sounds were gone.

When asked about the identity of the ghost, Kathy honestly admits that she has no idea who he could have been. Many possibilities offer themselves, including the soul of a man who hanged himself just outside the lighthouse.

Whoever he may be, the ghost has a long and active history. When crews were striving to repair the extensive damage done by a fire in 1971, workers experienced some frightening and mysterious incidents. A ceiling beam, one that should have been completely secure, fell on a worker. In another freak accident, a piece of wood struck a man's face. And a third worker was sent flying through the window of a truck after mysteriously being thrown from a tree. Many people, including the victims of the accidents, believe that these horrible accidents were somehow caused by an angry phantom.

The hostile force may have been caused by an apparition that had been seen briefly by another worker on the project. This gruesome image was hanging lifeless from a noose in a rope tied to a supporting joist. The worker attested that the vision disappeared as quickly as it had appeared. That worker was certainly not the first person to have reported seeing the hanging man. According to present-day lighthouse staff, several people in the 1930s reported seeing the hanged man's dead body. By now, the aura of evil seems to have lessened, but people still occasionally report feeling very uneasy near the site of the fire.

The phantom footsteps that crunch along in gravel might, understandably, feed that uneasy feeling. Those ghostly footsteps could be connected to the apparition frequently seen at one of the windows in the lighthouse. He is generally thought to be the ghost of a former keeper who is returning, after death, to continue the work that he did on earth. His specter has most often been noted in the "watcher's room," one floor below the actual light. Today, the room has been preserved as something of a living museum.

While in the watcher's room, staff members have frequently heard footsteps climbing up the winding staircase inside the tower. Of course, when one or another of the staff members hear this, they expect that they will have a visitor very shortly. Often, though, no one arrives with those sounds and when the concerned lighthouse worker goes to the stairs to see who might have been coming up, he or she finds that no one else is in the building and that he is alone, except perhaps for the haunting company of the soul of a former keeper who, years ago, fell to his death from the tower.

The least frightening manifestation at the lighthouse is the ghost of a little girl wearing a red dress. She's most often heard as she sings and chatters away across the veil of time, but occasionally she has also been seen. The child is thought to be the spirit of one of two sisters who lived at the lighthouse with their parents in 1873. The girls were apparently swept into the sea and their bodies were never recovered.

Everyone always knows when the spirit of former lighthouse keeper Joseph Andreu is about because the smell of cigar smoke suddenly fills the room. Andreu was working at the St. Augustine beacon in the 1870s when he met an accidental death.

All these hauntings have been well documented in books and on film for television shows. Today the light at the St. Augustine lighthouse is functioning once again, and the haunted installation on Anastasia Island is open to the public.

Ghost lovers are especially welcome.

Herman's Alone Now

For nearly 15 years in late 1800s, John Herman was a keeper at one of the most isolated lighthouses on the Great Lakes. The Waugoshance Lighthouse stands forlornly on a concrete pillar in an eastern part of Lake Michigan, miles from any other land mass. Anyone serving at the post would have to enjoy being alone.

When he first accepted responsibility for the light, John Herman might have enjoyed the forced, nearly complete isolation, but records indicate that eventually he turned to an over-indulgence in alcohol in his loneliness. Not surprisingly, being drunk on such a small spot of land, surrounded by the depths of Lake Michigan, eventually (probably in 1901) led to Herman's demise by drowning. He was last seen, very drunk, trying to make his way along the ledge of the concrete surrounding the beacon.

It was shortly after that sad accident that the assistant keepers at the Waugoshance Lighthouse began to notice odd occurrences. One night, for instance, when a lighthouse keeper fell asleep on the job, the chair on which he was reclining suddenly seemed to be kicked out from under him. On other occasions, boilers were stoked and buckets of coal filled when no one had been near them. Although all these phantom happenings were helpful, they were also frightening to anyone on duty and some say that, from that time on, keeper after keeper resigned from the position. Those who hold to this theory believe that word of a haunting at the lighthouse spread through the lighthouse keepers' community and no one would accept a posting there.

Be that as it may, the original, and very isolated, Waugoshance Lighthouse was abandoned in 1913. Today, close to 100 years later, it is still standing—crumbling from within and no doubt still haunted by the ghost of John Herman.

Lighthouse Snippets

So many haunted lighthouses dot the world's shores that one could not be blamed for wondering if any of those beacons are without at least some extra "spirit."

Gurnet Light

The Gurnet Light in Plymouth, Massachusetts, is haunted by the ghost of Hannah Thomas. John Thomas, Hannah's husband, had been the lighthouse keeper there for many years. For this reason, one might think that she haunts the light because it was a place where she was happiest but, apparently, her ghostly image is the picture of sadness. Some sorrow she endured in this world has, sadly, followed her into the next.

Point Lookout Light

Point Lookout Light on Chesapeake Bay, Maryland, is said to have been haunted since the 1860s. That ghost is also the wife of a lightkeeper. Her name, in life, was Ann Davis. It is likely that she was a busy soul when she was of this world because many people have become aware of her presence. Her voice has apparently even been captured on audio tape. Mrs. Davis is probably not a lonely entity because shortly after she returned to haunt the place where she lived in this life, she was joined by the ghosts of soldiers from the Civil War. People who have seen these military manifestations around the lighthouse suspect that they might be looking for their own graves—graves that were moved more than 100 years ago.

Ram Island

Two spirits, a man and a woman, are said to haunt the lighthouse on Ram Island in Boothbay Harbor, Maine. This pair, whose identity is unknown, clearly understands the purpose of a lighthouse, for they have been seen signaling sailors away from dangerous, submerged rocks near the shore.

Cape Lookout

A man named Joe Reynolds of North Carolina testifies that his daughter and his nephew approached the lighthouse at Cape Lookout, an unmanned station on a small North Carolina island. The two young people needed assistance and had seen a man standing by one of the lighthouse windows. The two young people knocked on the door to the lighthouse. Someone on the other side of that door knocked back at them but no one opened it for them. Whose figure they saw or who did the knocking has remained a mystery because, at that time, there was no one but themselves on the outcropping of land.

Bird Island

If you should happen to visit the Bird Island Lighthouse in Massachusetts' Buzzard's Bay, try to avoid cold and stormy days unless, of course, you want to risk running into the ghost of Billy Moore's wife. Moore was a pirate and every bit as mean a man at home as he was at work. He treated his wife brutally, and the poor woman's only comfort was the pipe she loved to smoke. People who have seen the woman's specter describe her ghost as being "disfigured and tattered." She's easily identified, though, as she looks out onto the water with her "old corncob pipe clenched in her jaw."

White River Lighthouse

A poignant story accompanies the haunting of a light-house near Whitehall, Michigan. Legend has it that Captain William Robinson and his beloved wife, Sara, spent most of their married lives as keepers of the White River Lighthouse. Finally authorities informed Robinson that the time had come—he must retire. That very night he died in his sleep, at the lighthouse he loved—never having had to obey the orders to leave the place. As a matter of fact, reports indicate that, to date, neither he nor Sara has ever left the light they both loved.

St. Simons Lighthouse

Phantom footfalls are sometimes heard ascending the stairs at the St. Simons Lighthouse on St. Simons Island in Georgia. The ghost with the heavy step is thought to be that of Frederick Osborne, who was murdered at that spot in 1880.

New London Ledge Lighthouse

A somewhat fanciful ghost legend exists about a ghost haunting the New London Ledge Lighthouse in New London, Connecticut. The spirit is said to be that of Ernie. Ernie and his wife were once responsible for the beacon but his wife, rumor has it, left Ernie for another man. The poor jilted husband threw himself from the tower and his heartbroken spirit seems intent on staying right there into its eternity. Ernie is said to unlock and open the door to the lens room when no one else is around and to sound the fog horn on clear days. He has even been accused of setting boats adrift that have been lashed to the pier at the base of the lighthouse.

Seul Choix Point Lighthouse

All that remains of Captain James Townsend's spirit, which apparently haunts the Seul Choix Point Lighthouse on Lake Michigan near Gulliver, Michigan, is the smell of the man's ever-present cigarettes. Although he was not associated with the place for most of his life, Townsend was taken there when he was deathly ill. He didn't recover from his sickness but died at the lighthouse and his body was stored there for several days. The body is, of course, gone now, but the smoky smell from the man's cigarettes can still occasionally be detected.

Boon Island Lighthouse

Pity poor Katherine Bright. The bride was forced to stay alone with her new husband's corpse at the Boon Island Light near York in Maine. She was totally demented by the time she was found and never breathed a sane breath again in her life. In death she has returned to that lighthouse—the place of her terrible sorrow.

Seguin Island Lighthouse

Ghosts have haunted the Seguin Island Lighthouse for nearly 200 years. As with many legends about lighthouse ghosts, this one implies that the total isolation inherent in such a posting had a deadly effect on both the keeper and his wife.

The lighthouse keeper's quarters at Boon Island in Maine

Sometime in the 1800s, it is said, a couple lived at this beacon near Popham Beach in Maine. It is likely that the wife was the first to react to the terrible loneliness. She was an accomplished pianist who may have given up a professional career on the performing stage in order to be with her husband. Perhaps she thought that being a hermit for a period of time would give her plenty of time to polish her musical skills. And, for some time, perhaps it did. As the years wore on, however, the woman became less and less emotionally stable, eventually spiraling downward to the point that she only played one piece of music—over and over again.

Rather than seek help for his suffering wife, the man, who had likely become somewhat unstable himself at this point, sneaked up behind her one day when she was sitting at the piano. As he slowly and quietly made his way toward her he was hiding the ax he was carrying. She didn't seem to sense her husband's approach. The man was so close to his wife that he could feel the heat from her back against his body. Still she didn't stop playing that one dreadful tune. She didn't even look away from the piano keys.

He raised the ax up above his head and gave it one heavy swing downward. Instantly, his wife lay dead, blood coursing out onto the piano and its bench. Seconds later the lifeless body slumped to the floor beside her beloved musical instrument.

On calm nights, people walking near that lightkeeper's house have heard the sounds of a piano being played. Usually when they do hear such music, folks don't dawdle but tend to scurry away. Not only do they know that they are not hearing music of this dimension, but the tune being played soon becomes extremely annoying for it is the same song—being played over and over again.

Pemaquid Point Lighthouse

At the shoreline near the Pemaquid Point Lighthouse near Bristol Maine, it is said that you can hear the cries of the sailors who lost their lives when the ships they were on foundered below. Occasionally, people report seeing the filmy image of a young woman walking near the water. Anyone who sees her knows immediately that she is not from this world, for she seems to be walking not on but just above the rocks. Perhaps her soul is searching for the love of her earthly life. Perhaps he was one of the many sailors who have met their death against that shore.

4
Derelicts

*E*ven an abandoned building is an eerie sight, inviting speculation about why the place should have been deserted and what—physical or metaphysical—might have been left behind when the structure was vacated. The sight of an abandoned ship, a vessel floating aimlessly about, devoid of people, is nothing short of creepy!

The Crew That Vanished

Human beings are highly social creatures. We need other people. This basic need is dramatically revealed by the recurring nightmare many people experience—that they are absolutely alone in the world. Authors and screenplay writers often take advantage of our fear of being alone. When they want to set up a scene that all their readers or viewers will find spooky, they often depict a solitary soul walking through a deserted town or city. To find *no one* where we expect *someone* is distinctly unnerving. When there are signs that the missing person had been in the middle of a mundane activity, such as eating breakfast, before suddenly vanishing, the scene becomes downright sinister.

Situations that combine this fear and curiosity are compelling. This is no doubt one of the reasons legends of derelict ships—ships that have been found in sailing condition but abandoned—have become engraved in the annals of our paranormal history.

The story of the *Mary Celeste* has become such a spooky, classic seafaring legend that to exclude telling the story in this book would be a terrible omission.

A long-standing belief among members of the sailing community is that changing a ship's name will bring bad luck to not only the vessel but also to all those associated with her. The following account certainly supports that theory.

The ship we know as the *Mary Celeste* was first known as the *Amazon* when it was built in a shipyard in Nova Scotia, Canada, in 1861. Seven years later, her first owners

When the Mary Celeste *sailed for Genoa, Italy, no one could have imagined the bizarre outcome of her voyage.*

sold her to an American firm that renamed her the *Mary Sellars*. Specifics are cloudy at this point, but sometime between then and 1872, when the ill-fated skipper Captain Briggs took over her command, the *Mary Sellars* finally became the *Mary Celeste*.

On November 5, 1872, both the square-rigged *Mary Celeste* and later the *Dei Gratia* departed from the port of New York City on November 5, 1872. A month later, the crew of the *Dei Gratia* discovered the *Mary Celeste* abandoned at a point roughly midway between Portugal and the Azores. Her intended voyage to Genoa, Italy, had obviously been permanently interrupted. Her cargo of unrefined alcohol was undelivered and her crew, including the captain, his wife and daughter, were all missing.

Oddly, the more closely this century-old riddle of the deserted ship is examined, the more puzzling it becomes. For those with weak research skills or no sense of a mystery, the solution can easily be found. Folks with such a bent would probably say, "The hull of the *Celeste* showed signs of damage and she had taken on water and the ship's lifeboat was missing. It's evident she ran up against an uncharted obstacle and the captain, fearing the ship would sink, ordered everyone into the lifeboat which, not surprisingly, capsized in the waves of the Atlantic Ocean."

It takes very little investigation to sink that over-simplified explanation, because the story of the *Mary Celeste* is a tale of contradictions that becomes more, rather than less, confusing under close scrutiny.

Captain Benjamin Spooner Briggs, age 37, was an experienced sailor. Married to a woman named Sarah, Briggs was the father of a toddler, Sophia. Theirs must have been a close little family, close enough that, as he steered the bow of the *Mary Celeste* from its home port in the autumn of 1872, Briggs' wife and daughter were also on board.

Albert Richardson served as first mate for the trip, leading a well-experienced crew of seven sailors. If they anticipated anything out of the ordinary during this sailing, it was not recorded at any point in the captain's meticulously kept logbook. Apparently, they traveled uneventfully along their charted course from early November until November 24, when they were hit by a severe storm.

"We are in sight of the Azores," Captain Briggs noted in his log that day. "A storm approaches. Have furled some sails."

The next day's logbook entry was unusually brief, consisting only of the ship's bearings. Those figures were Captain Briggs' final notation.

Ten days later, the English ship *Dei Gratia*, under Captain David Morehouse's command, caught sight of what appeared to be a ship off in the distance. Initially, Morehouse was understandably unconcerned. With so many other ships traversing the seas, coming across another vessel during any voyage was a common event. An hour later, it became clear that there was something very different about this morning's sighting. The ship they were approaching appeared to be floating aimlessly, as directionless as a cork bobbing about on the sea.

Morehouse altered the *Dei Gratia*'s course slightly in order to get sufficiently close to investigate the situation. When he felt it was safe to do so, the captain launched a longboat, manned with three of his sailors who were under orders to check out the other ship and report their findings back to Morehouse.

"Ahoy, ahoy!" the concerned sailors likely cried out as they made their way onto the deck of the *Mary Celeste*. "We've come to offer aid. Are you in distress here?"

The three men listened for a reply but were rewarded with total silence. Cautiously, they began to explore the drifting craft. Some of the ship's sails hung in tatters on the masts. The small boarding party peered tentatively below deck, no doubt expecting to find corpses below.

Surely old man Morehouse won't make us bring their bodies aboard, a ship's mate named Wright may have thought hopefully as he and his two mates descended into the *Mary Celeste*'s quarters. Every sailor knew that carrying a deceased person could bring terribly bad luck to a ship for years to come. Carrying an entire crew of corpses would surely jinx all on board the *Dei Gratia* for the rest of their lives.

"I'll suggest we leave the bodies right where they are and tow this vessel back to port. He knows the legends of the sea even better than we do, so maybe he'll agree," first mate Deveau may have assured Wright to allay his fears.

But the trio from the *Dei Gratia* did not find the bodies of Captain Briggs, his wife, his daughter, his first mate or any of the crew. They found no one on board the *Mary Celeste*. No one at all—neither living nor deceased. As the boarding sailors' eyes slowly adjusted to the darkness below the *Mary Celeste*'s deck, and their minds adjusted to the all-encompassing emptiness surrounding them, the three scouts looked about, assessing the strange scenes that greeted them.

Little Sophia's toys lay spread out across her parents' bed as though she had been playing with them only seconds before she mysteriously departed her father's ship. Sophia's mother, a music lover, had brought her rosewood melodeon (an old-fashioned stringed instrument) with her on the voyage. Sheet music for the instrument lay open as though something had interrupted someone's playing.

In the crew's cabin, laundry was hung tidily on lines and other clothing lay folded on bunks. It was the scene in the galley, though, that unnerved the sailors the most. Breakfast appeared to have been served because the captain's soft-boiled eggs still rested in egg cups, the tops of their shells removed in anticipation of the eggs being eaten and enjoyed by a man with a hearty appetite.

Understandably eager to flee from these unnatural surroundings, the sailors from the *Dei Gratia* made for the longboat and steered it back to their own ship as quickly as they were able. They gave Captain Morehouse the details of their strange findings. He responded in the way they'd hoped he would. Rather than risking bringing any hidden corpses onto their ship, the *Dei Gratia*'s crew prepared to tow the *Celeste* into the closest harbor— Gibraltar.

During that trip, Morehouse likely ran the details of the strange scenario he'd happened upon, over and over in his mind. The storm to which Captain Briggs referred in his final log notation may have become so severe that he decided to abandon ship. But that was not a decision an experienced skipper such as Briggs was likely to have made. If the storm were severe enough to threaten the safety of those aboard the brigantine, Briggs certainly wouldn't have tried to ride it out in a lifeboat. As well, ample evidence lay below the *Mary Celeste*'s deck suggest a hasty abandonment. A bottle stood on a counter, its top off but its contents intact. Small, light ornaments that would have been easily disturbed stood on shelves, unmoved and unbroken. And what of the eggs in the egg cups? All natural laws deem that if the *Mary Celeste* had weathered a storm severe enough to make an experienced sea captain leave his ship, then his breakfast could not have remained stationary at his place at the table. No reasonable theory could be created from the available evidence.

The sextant, an important nautical instrument, was missing from the *Mary Celeste*, yet all the crew's personal effects, including money and papers, remained on the ship. Odder still was the condition of the ship's compass. It had been smashed heavily enough that the stand on which it belonged had been knocked away from its usual position.

Had the crew succumbed to the temptations of their intoxicating cargo? Some versions of the legend say that nine of the 1701 casks of alcohol were bone dry, completely empty of the cargo that Briggs had been transporting across the Atlantic. Despite that fact, the intoxication theory is not logical because the *Mary Celeste* was still neat and orderly. No signs indicated that there had been any sort of drunkenness on board the craft. No, the missing alcohol did not solve the mystery—it complicated it.

Many more questions than answers were at hand. For example, one of the cabins had been hastily boarded up. Why? No clue was left behind to provide a possible answer.

Most puzzling of all is the question of how the ship came to be where the *Dei Gratia* found it. At Captain Briggs' last entry, the ship had been on course and the sails set accordingly—tacking to port. By the time Morehouse and his men found the *Mary Celeste*, wind conditions had changed and the *Dei Gratia* was tacking to starboard, the only way she could have arrived at the spot where the abandoned ship sat. The *Mary Celeste* could not have traveled the 500 miles she had, in the direction she did, merely by floating for the 10 days between the captain's last log entry and the *Dei Gratia* crew's discovery.

But it apparently had.

The *Dei Gratia*, towing the deserted brig behind it, made its way uneventfully to Gibraltar. In accordance with centuries-old salvage laws of seafaring, Morehouse expected to be awarded the profits from the sale of his discovered booty. However, Lloyd's of London, who insured the *Mary Celeste*, investigated the derelict and determined, to their satisfaction, that the cargo had ignited a flash fire in one of the holds. Knowing the properties of alcohol, the insurance company assumed that Briggs and the others fled the ship, intending to return once the fire extinguished itself. The company further hypothesized that, for some unknown reason, those nine souls were prevented from reboarding the vessel and were lost at sea. Battles over who should claim the insurance money raged for years.

Interestingly, the insurer's investigation also determined that, although there were sufficient stores of food and water remaining, a deadly bacteria had developed in the bread. Scientists were aware that eating food infected with the fungus would eventually cause death but, before it killed, it caused a madness that was horrible to watch. Perhaps, one by one, the crew had succumbed to the effects of the mind-altering mold and together, in their crazed states, decided they needed to abandon the *Mary Celeste*.

History has not tracked the career of *Dei Gratia*'s Captain Morehouse from this point on. We can surmise that he saw some profit from his find. Whether or not he led a peaceful or prosperous existence is not known. However, the remaining years for the abandoned ship Morehouse had towed to harbor just before Christmas of 1872 were anything but peaceful and prosperous.

Even though the *Mary Celeste* had sustained only minimal damage, and it was readily repaired, subsequent owners of the craft were plagued with ill fortune. Sailors who could find work on other vessels refused to sail on the *Celeste*, saying she was cursed, jinxed, a hoodoo ship. This left her manned by woefully inadequate crews, sailors no one else wanted to employ.

The *Mary Celeste* went through almost 20 owners in its remaining years of service. She sailed, in increasing states of economic and physical decline, for another 12 years. She was finally destroyed off the shores of Haiti when she was run aground, some say purposely, by her last captain.

Controversy swirling around the *Mary Celeste* has never completely becalmed itself. Some people felt that the captain and crew of the *Dei Gratia* had waited until the *Celeste* was in an isolated position, then boarded her and murdered everyone. This theory begs the question "why?" for nothing of value was stolen.

Others have suspected that Captain Briggs and Captain Morehouse plotted the entire scheme in order to profit from the insurance claims that would result. This is unlikely because both Briggs and Morehouse had many years of profitable employment ahead of them— too much to throw away on such a criminal plan.

We do know that great misfortune followed the ship for every one of her remaining days at sea. Perhaps the souls of Captain Briggs and the others remained on board to haunt the ship in the hopes of drawing attention to their mysterious demise.

If it was attention that those aboard the *Mary Celeste* were after, then their souls must, by now, be gratified. Right from the earliest report of this derelict, the story has fascinated people. Even Arthur Conan Doyle, Sherlock Holmes' creator, took a crack at solving the mystery in a short story involving an abandoned ship that he transparently named the *Marie Celeste*. Since then, more than 30 books have been written about the mystery of the *Mary Celeste* and, more recently, both documentary and feature films have also been made. It is a haunting sea story that we who love mysteries will apparently not let die.

An up-to-date postscript exists for this old story: the ship's rotting hulk. Scientist and author Dr. Clive Cussler led an expedition in the summer of 2001 that finally found the rotting remains of the *Mary Celeste*. In his considered opinion, "The true story of her missing crew may never be known."

The mystery of the *Mary Celeste* will, therefore, continue to haunt us.

Little Jewel's Big Mystery

The following true tale rivals that of the *Mary Celeste* as an absolute mystery and the *Great Eastern* for bad luck.

The *Joyita* (Little Jewel) had been built in 1931 in a Los Angeles shipyard as a yacht for Hollywood film producer Roland West. She was named after West's friend Jewel Carmen. When the luxury yacht was completed, it was readied to be rolled out for launching. Tragically, a shipwright who had recently emigrated from Portugal fell from the boat onto the guide rails below and died instantly. All connected with the floating palace knew at that instant that the craft's future of bad luck had been established with that one fatal accident.

They did not expect their prediction to be realized so quickly. The very next morning the worker's widow came running to the dock where the yacht was being launched. The woman was hysterical with grief and began screaming that her husband had died as a direct result of unsafe work conditions brought on by the shipyard's desire to finish the job too quickly.

All attempts to calm and comfort the woman were ineffective and eventually she was carried off by authorities. As she was being taken away in restraints she turned her body back around so that she was facing the vessel that had caused her terrible agony. In Portuguese, her native language, she shouted a curse at the boat and then fell silent.

It didn't take long for word of that incident to spread throughout the California shipyard community. No one

who didn't absolutely have to would go near the brand-new
Joyita.

Less than a year later the friendship between Jewel and
West had soured. A few months later, on what should have
been an idyllic cruise to Catalina Island, an unexplained
fire broke out in the yacht's engine room. Damage was
extensive and expensive. Soon, she was sold and turned
into a charter yacht.

In this incarnation, the cursed *Joyita* carried some of
Hollywood's most famous actors and actresses. As nothing untoward happened during any of those voyages it
seemed that the power of the curse had expired. The boat,
once again, began to appeal to private owners. Both
Humphrey Bogart and Errol Flynn (who not long after
did buy a yacht—and a haunted one at that) were interested in buying the *Joyita* until it became known that a
passenger had mysteriously disappeared from the boat
during one of her routine trips to Catalina Island.

A few years after that, the United States became
involved in World War II, and the *Joyita* was seconded and
sent to Pearl Harbor as a patrol boat. She proved to be
more trouble than she was worth because, despite experienced captains at her helm, she ran aground an inordinate
number of times. Finally authorities sent her to the bone-
yard. The owners who had used her as a charter ship were
no longer interested in owning her and so they sold her
for little more than scrap.

As the *Joyita*'s once-luxurious fittings were scavenged
for parts she became, effectively, a ghost of her former
self. It was then that it became apparent that even in this
deteriorated state, the woman's curse still echoed through

her hull. In 1947, while on board the craft, a man was overcome with battery acid fumes and died.

Not long after that and for reasons never identified, the *Joyita* broke loose from her moorings. She floated out to clear water where she collided with another ship, damaging both vessels. After being towed back into harbor and re-tied, two drunken sailors from a nearby ship boarded her. Their drunken camaraderie, if they ever had any, evaporated like vapors of alcohol and they began arguing. The argument turned physical and not long after both men lay dead on the *Joyita*'s deck.

Incredibly, the former yacht was then stripped of almost all her fittings and turned into a cargo ship. She was serving in this capacity when, on October 3, 1955, she was found abandoned near the paradise of Western Samoa. She had been carrying a load of lumber as well as 25 people—a crew of six capable sailors, including her captain, a World War II veteran named Thomas ("Dusty") Miller, nine laborers and nine passengers.

The *Tuvala*, an inter-island freighter under the command of Captain Gerald Douglas, boarded the derelict *Joyita* and conducted a cursory search before towing her to port. Once there the hoodoo ship was searched from stem to stern. No one, alive or dead, was found. No messages of any sort had been left by those who had been aboard her except that the vessel's signal flags had been carefully arranged to display the letters WNQV. Unfortunately, this meant nothing to anyone, even those with extensive marine knowledge.

The clocks aboard had both stopped at exactly two minutes before ten. The cook stove was set to the "on" position as were all the switches and controls used to operate the vessel. To add to the mystery, the captain's logbook was missing, as were the cargo, the life rafts and some very heavy metal cargo. It was just not reasonable to think that another craft, large enough to create this enigma at sea, could have been in the area without authorities being aware. What on earth could have happened?

The investigations that followed were thorough but not satisfying. The only suspicious piece of information that emerged was the news that, on the day the *Joyita* last set out, a woman ran toward the boat screaming for her nephew, a member of the crew, to leave the ship while there was still time. She claimed to somehow know that this sailing was not going to end well, that the boat was under an evil curse.

Several years later, *Life* magazine carried an article about the jinxed *Joyita*. In it Captain Dusty Miller admitted that he had frequently sighted what looked to have been, impossibly, a Portuguese galleon from Columbus' era following the *Joyita* as she made her voyages. That grieving widow's curse never lost its control over the ill-fated boat.

At last report, the abandoned, jinxed and ruined vessel had been bought by a museum. As such places are often haunted by the pasts of many of their artifacts, it is hoped that the hulk's harmful powers had finally subsided.

Shocking Discovery

If deserted towns are called ghost towns, then should deserted ships be called ghost ships? Apparently not, since the term "ghost ship" in naval lore describes an apparition of a vessel that foundered tragically long ago.

Instead, a deserted ship that still physically exists is called a derelict. Such a vessel may or may not be haunted by the ghosts of her sailors but even if she is not, seeing a derelict must be a deeply disturbing experience. Such wrecks have been found all over the world but most often in frozen waters.

In 1775, a whaling ship called the *Herald* was working just off the west coast of Greenland. At one point in the expedition the vessel was becalmed. While the captain, a man named Warren, and his crew sat out the still weather, a sight they would certainly never forget was revealed to them—an empty and unfamiliar ship.

When the strange craft would not reply to signals from the *Herald,* Captain Warren ordered that a boarding party from his ship be loaded into a lifeboat and sent out to investigate this unusual circumstance.

As the scouts came near the unknown ship, they were able to read the name. Although the letters were badly faded, the word "Octavius" was spelled out on the side of the ship. The men from the *Herald* called out greetings to anyone who might have been aboard the *Octavius*. When no one replied to their calls, the small group boarded the ship. What they found below the vessel's deck was nothing short of a nightmare. A row of frozen bodies lined the sailors' quarters. Next door in the captain's cabin lay four more corpses—those of the captain, his wife and child as well as that of a sailor.

No sign of the *Octavius* was ever seen again. Interestingly, though, she was probably the first ship to make her way through the Northwest Passage—although, at the time of that accomplishment all of those on board were there in body only. They had been dead for many, many months.

Phantom Ship of the Arctic

The *Baychimo*'s last voyage was a race she did not win. The ship was owned by the Hudson's Bay Company. She had served the company well, year after year making the 2000-mile round trip from Vancouver, British Columbia, to the Arctic, where she delivered supplies and picked up loads of furs from northern trappers.

Each trip was dangerous, a challenging quest for the crew and hard on the ship itself. The *Baychimo*'s last challenge, the one she lost, began early in July 1931 when Captain John Cornwell and a crew of three dozen well-qualified sailors headed out of Vancouver's harbor. By the end of September she was homeward bound, but soon enough ice had formed to block her progress. Worse, a glimpse at the horizon indicated that a vicious storm was approaching.

The one good circumstance was that the ship and all aboard were still within view of the village of Barrow, Alaska, where the Hudson's Bay Company had established hut-like shelters. The men went to these shelters and survived two miserable days and nights in those

The specter of the Baychimo, *which vanished without explanation in 1931, still haunts the icy Arctic waters.*

accommodations before a small miracle occurred. On October 4, the ice jammed up against the *Baychimo* suddenly fell back from the ship.

Their hearts soaring, the men ran back to the craft and resumed their journey homeward. They didn't know what strange event had freed their vessel and saved them from being stranded on the tundra. They were just grateful that it had.

Their luck held, but for only a few days. By October 8 the *Baychimo*, with all hands on board, was frozen in the ice once again. The men were able to radio their distress to the closest airport, and planes were dispatched to rescue as many of those stranded as possible. Twenty-two men were airlifted to safety, leaving only the ship's captain and 14 others behind to wait for the next flight—which might well not come for an entire year.

Those left behind set about making sure that they lasted the year. Taking wood from the ship, they built a shelter on the ice near the ship and huddled in there until mid-November when a blizzard buried them, building and all. By the time the 15 weakened men had dug themselves out their ship, the *Baychimo* had vanished. They searched for her for a while but soon presumed that the ship had sunk—valuable cargo and all. She had no doubt broken to bits under the crush of the ice and the storm. At that point there was no reason to stay where they were, so the stranded men trekked inland to safety.

As they waited out the rest of the season in safety, the men heard a report that Inuit fishermen had seen the *Baychimo* floating about in an ice jam not too far from where she'd disappeared from the crew's sight. They rushed to the direction they'd been given and, sure enough, there she was—intact but tightly frozen in place. The 15 men boarded her and salvaged as many of the furs as they were able to. Not long after, they were picked up by a rescue aircraft and flown south again just grateful to have lived through the endeavor.

The next person to see the *Baychimo*'s frozen hull was a trapper named Leslie Melvin, who boarded the ship in March 1932. He found the remains of the valuable furs still on board but had to leave them there because he had no way of carrying them out.

A full year later the derelict was seen again—this time in almost exactly the same spot where she'd been abandoned. Wanting to claim the furs, the group that had found her tried to board the *Baychimo*. They failed, for just as they came close to her, a tremendous storm blew out of seemingly nowhere and prevented them from getting any closer to the potentially valuable cache.

Stories about this eerily resilient derelict spread around the world. She was boarded again, for a short period of time, in the summer of 1934, but her cargo was not touched. She was reportedly seen again, still in one piece, during September 1935.

As one person with a fascination for this strange series of events wrote, "Nature seemed unable to destroy her, but man was equally unable to rescue her."

Locals became less and less surprised to see the floating derelict from time to time. Others had a more specific interest in the ship's integrity. Those people wanted to salvage and profit from the stash of pelts stowed on board. They also failed, as they were unable to take enough pelts to make the attempt worth the risk.

The ship was seen again floating in the Beaufort Sea during March 1962. No one approached her that time. The last recorded sighting of this eerily and almost miraculously preserved vessel was also in the Beaufort Sea—in 1968— nearly 40 years after she'd been abandoned.

As for the ship's owners, the Hudson's Bay Company, their official stance is that they do not know whether their formerly reliable cargo ship might still be sailing— crewless—into the great beyond or not. They do know that when they hear tales about the gray ghost in the Arctic, people are referring to their ship—the possibly unnaturally preserved *Baychimo*.

5
Strange and Spooky Sea Stories

As the following strange and spooky tales demonstrate, some ghost stories of the sea refuse to be neatly categorized.

Angry Presence

Pirate legends often romanticize the exploits of these murderers and thieves, but pirates were often so dishonest that they even robbed from one another. So much for the theory about honor among thieves. A rowdy group of buccaneers, with not a speck of honor among them, under the guidance of a particularly evil pirate named Archie, landed on a beach near Charleston, South Carolina. Their ship's hold was filled with jewels, coins, precious metals and firearms—loot stolen from a Spanish pirate. Archie and his men intended to divide the riches and use the profits to help them settle in the "new world."

First, though, they decided that they owed themselves a celebration, so they broke open casks of alcohol and began to drink and dance and fight in frenzied delight to acknowledge their proud, albeit dishonest, accomplishments. Unfortunately, they became so involved with their riotous partying that none of them noticed a ship approaching.

When someone finally did spot the vessel, Archie, who was far from sober by that time, did his best to see that his treasures were hidden. He was sure that the men on the ship sailing toward them would try to steal the riches that he and his men had sailed safely to the Carolina coast. He declared in a loud and drunken voice that anyone wanting to get to his booty would have to "get past me, dead or alive."

Less than a day later, Archie's beaten and bloodied body lay on the beach beside the bodies of most of his men. He and his crew of pirates must have done a better job of stashing the loot than fighting off the enemy because, despite their best efforts, the invaders were unable to find the hidden cache. Eventually they gave up and set sail once again, leaving the bodies of their victims to rot on the sands.

Soon after, word began to get around that there was buried treasure in the area and that whoever found it would become extremely wealthy. People desperate to improve their financial lot in life came from near and far. They tore up the area but never found so much as a trinket and, after a while, these people abandoned the project.

Military men from a nearby base were the next to try their hands at the "get rich quick" scheme. They organized and equipped themselves before setting out on their mission. They decided to dig where the other treasure hunters had not. As they forced their shovels into the ground, one soldier screamed at the top of his lungs before fainting dead away. His workmates ran to help the felled man, but their attention was soon diverted—to a transparent image of an exceptionally ugly man. One soldier approached the huge figure while the rest of the men tended to their fallen friend. As the man was walking toward the unnaturally large manifestation, an earthquake of unusually strong proportions shook the ground below them. The soldiers fled in terror, vowing never to return to the area. And they never did.

In years following, others eager for "easy" financial gains were not so wise. All who searched near one particular spot on the beach were scared away by a huge and slightly transparent vision of a pirate. His cold eyes struck terror in the hearts of anyone who saw his spirit.

The last recorded party of treasure hunters to see the pirate's ghost landed on the beach just as the skies suddenly darkened. As they came ashore, the waves began to pound the shore but the seekers were too greedy to be warned off by such signs. They wanted the buried treasure. They made their way, carrying picks and shovels, determined to work come rain or shine—until an enormous man suddenly appeared from nowhere. With his fists jammed against his hips and his sword at his waist, the long-deceased pirate made a formidable phantom.

As one, the men fled back to their boat, but the storm that had come on so suddenly as they landed had now worsened considerably. No trace of any of the men, or their ship, was ever found. It was widely presumed that they were lost in the vicious storm while trying to flee from the ghost.

Archie's soul has apparently made good on the man's dying threat. Anyone who wants to get at his treasure will have to get past him—or his ghost. To date, no one has been able to do that.

Ancient Enigma

The following true tale has neither a ghost nor the sea in it but it is as mysterious as any ghost story I've ever been told and it involves a ship. That is how it made its way into this book.

☠

It was 1933 when Louis and Myrtle Botts were hiking in a portion of California's Imperial Valley that is now called Desert State Park. They were amateur botanists who lived in the nearby town of Julian and were interested in wildflowers. They walked through this particular spot often because of its exceptionally rich cache of small flowering plants.

The pair had been enjoying the wonderfully fresh air, the pretty blooms, the gorgeous scenery and each other's company for about an hour when they noticed a man approaching them. He was rather disheveled looking, and for a moment, the Botts were concerned for their safety. Soon, though, it became apparent that the man was simply an old prospector. As the man approached the couple, he waved and called out to them.

Myrtle tugged on the sleeve of her husband's shirt and whispered, "He must want to talk to us."

Louis assured her that, at second glance, the strange old fellow looked harmless enough. Without hesitating, the pair approached him.

"My name's Jake," the fellow announced. "And I've just seen the most amazing sight. There's the hull of an old ship sticking out of the mountainside back there a piece!"

Neither Myrtle nor Louis knew how to reply. They merely nodded mutely. Surely what this man claimed to have seen was not possible. As the Botts stood staring at the prospector, Jake continued talking. "But, that's not all. I've found the Peg Leg Smith's lost mine."

Now both Myrtle and Louis knew that the man had been out in the sun and the sand of the canyon too long. Everyone knew that the lost mine was a myth, that no such thing really existed. The Botts also knew that the man who'd introduced himself as Jake, and who had told them this amazing story about a ship jutting out from a mountain wall, was just another desert rat. All such hermit-like folks eventually went completely crazy. Myrtle and Louis thanked the man as politely as they could, bid him a good day and quickly took their leave.

"Poor soul," Myrtle said as they neared home. "He's completely lost touch with reality."

The next day the Botts headed out once again into the canyon. This time they got a little farther, past a steep grade in the trail. They no sooner crested the hill than Louis stopped dead in his tracks. There, high above them, jutting out from the mountainside, was the enormous bow of an ancient ship.

At first they stared in disbelief at the curved hull and the round marks on the side facing them where shields must once have been attached as protection. Impossibly, at least it seemed so to the Botts, this seagoing relic was lodged between layers and layers of clay and shale. Myrtle and Louis carefully memorized the location of this strange artifact and then hurried back home to mark the location on a map.

They were no sooner clear of the canyon than the devastating earthquake of 1933 hit the area. The land for miles around was violently shaken and left tumultuously rearranged. The anomalous ship's hull was never seen again. Its disappearance, however, did not mean the end of Myrtle's interest in the origins of the bizarre sight she had been witness to. She began to research ancient ships and discovered that the hull she and her husband had seen in the Desert State Park resembled those vessels used by Norse explorers at the time of Leif Ericson.

This information only added to the Botts' puzzle. How could such a ship make its way over mountains and end up 40 miles inland? Myrtle knew she'd have to make a trip back to the canyon as soon as possible. This time she had a camera with her, so that if the wreck was visible she could take a picture of it. They were only able to get within sighting distance of the spot, because the quake had created a landslide that now blocked the trail. Even from where they stood though, Louis and Myrtle could tell that the ship was no longer visible.

Dreadfully disappointed and frustrated at having no proof of their amazing discovery, the couple returned home. Further research would have to serve as the proof that they'd wanted their snapshots to supply. And, to a large degree, the additional information that Myrtle Botts collected did, at least, support their assertions.

It seems that Norse people explored the California coast at a time (circa 900–1100 BCE) when the earth's temperatures were high and the Arctic ice cap was melting. It is thought that the Northwest Passage was open at that time. This would have created a direct route for explorers, and the prevailing winds of the area (easterlies) would have provided the power to get their vessels home again. In addition, many historical geographers are of the opinion that, in those days, the Gulf of Mexico extended into the Imperial Valley. If this was so, then the ship the Botts saw might just have run aground during one of the early Norse expeditions.

A legend among the natives of southern California and northern Mexico supports that premise. Thousands of years ago, it is said, those areas were visited by "Come-From-Afar-Men" aboard a "long boat with a head like a snake." These ancient visitors were said to have had red or light-colored hair and beards. If this sounds like a science fiction story to you, perhaps you'll be interested to know that even today the swarthy-skinned natives from those areas in California and Mexico will produce blond children with blue eyes. These statistically rare children may be descendents of "Come-From-Afar-Men"—in all likelihood, Norsemen.

And so, although this true story includes neither a ghost nor the sea, it is far too intriguing to leave out.

Killer Cur

Seeing a ghost frightens sailors. Seeing the ghost of an animal—especially the ghost of a black dog—can nearly paralyze an entire crew with terror. The ghost dog does not even have to be on board the ship in order for a terrible fright to take hold of boatmen, as the following incident at the harbor in Hull, England, bears out.

The phantom appeared near the docks every night at twilight. Whenever a sailor walked to, or from, his ship, the jet black ghost dog would follow—growling and snapping threats at anyone who was about. Once the angry apparition had done his job by thoroughly frightening whoever was on the dock, the cur would make his way back to a nearby lumberyard where his image would slowly vaporize—only to appear again when the next person dared to stroll along the wharf.

A sailor was quoted in the *London Daily Mail* as saying, "No one has ever seen the thing by day. The timber yard into which it vanishes has been searched from sunrise to sunset, but not a sign of it is ever seen until night."

He went on to reveal, "What is almost certain is that it brings death if it comes too near. Frank Robinson, a ship's fireman, saw it quite close. His body was found in the locks the next morning."

The association between Robinson's encountering the ghost and his death almost immediately afterward was reported to authorities, which apparently succeeded in spreading a sense of terror into the community itself.

"The thing was mentioned at the inquest, when the terror it has caused was even felt in court in broad daylight," according to a court official.

As for the sailors who still had to access their vessels via the haunted wharf, some were nearly insane with fear. Some left their lives at sea for land-bound careers. Others persevered but indicated that they "walked warily," especially after dark. Although no more deaths could be so directly linked to the presence of this evil canine spirit, those who saw the ghost "flash past, in the shadows of the docks" were restless and on edge until they were able to ship out of that seemingly jinxed and haunted English port.

As this haunting was reported about 60 years ago, we can hope that the dog's powers of manifestation have weakened by now and that the pier is no longer possessed.

Sailor's Grave

Occasionally, a paranormal manifestation will make the news. The following ghost story, for instance, was reported in the Rochester *Democrat and Chronicle* on May 12, 1921.

Up to that time, the area along the shores of Lake Ontario had been virtually untouched, having only ever been sparsely populated by aboriginal people and briefly explored by passing Europeans. Its raw, natural beauty must have been utterly breathtaking.

Of course, nature untamed can be as dangerous as it is beautiful and many premature deaths ensued in the 1800s and early 1900s. A sailor who had drowned during a storm in 1857 had been laid to rest on the shore of Point Charles in Sodus Bay, New York. By the early 1900s, the area was becoming populated with luxurious cottages and wealthy cottagers. Some of these cottage owners formed an association. As a group, they hired a caretaker to be responsible for the general maintenance and upkeep of the land around their rambling summer homes. In 1917, the caretaker was a man named George Carson.

Carson was familiar with the area. He knew, for instance, that some said that when a hard northeastern wind blew across Sodus Bay, the phantom cries of that long-deceased sailor buried near their cottages could be heard. Carson was a lifelong skeptic and was convinced that the sounds they reported were merely wind noises, and that the people's imaginations were turning the sounds into something they weren't.

Nor did Carson believe the Murphy family when they reported that they had been visited by a ghost during a severe northeastern storm. Although he liked and trusted the Murphys in all other regards, he could not put any credence in their recollections of that particular summer night. The family maintained that they were sitting at their dining room table when they heard knocking sounds coming from the outside their cottage walls. Mr. Murphy asserted that he looked out of every window in the house and that he couldn't see anyone or anything that could be making such sounds.

The homeowner ordered his children to stay quiet while the noisy phenomenon persisted. At first he thought the racket was caused by one of his neighbors playing a trick, but when the knocks continued for over 10 minutes, he decided that more action was necessary. Murphy and his children went out the back door of the cottage. Half of the group went to the right, the other half to the left. Soon they reunited at the front door, having seen nothing at all out of the ordinary nor anything that could have made the strange sounds.

The two youngest children quickly went back inside while Mr. Murphy and his older son continued to look around the outside of the house for clues as to what could have been making the knocking sounds. Despite the windstorm, the two men stayed outside until their determination was rewarded. There, down by the windswept lake, sitting on a bench, was a ghostly form. They watched in horror and amazement as the apparition stood up, walked over to the by now all-but-forgotten grave, raised its hands straight above its head and then disappeared.

Not one member of the Murphy family slept well that night, but everyone rose early. By noon the next day they had created a monument of stones and placed it over the gravesite. Perhaps this would keep the restless spirit from rising up and haunting them when the next northeasterly storm hit.

Later that summer, as George Carson was tending to the Murphys' property, he accidentally knocked over the headstone they had so carefully created and placed. Knowing that the grave itself was very old but *not* knowing about the family's recent experiences, Carson simply gathered up the stones with the other detritus from his lawn work and threw everything into the pile behind the cottages.

That evening, Carson took an after-dinner stroll in the twilight. As he approached the shoreline near the Murphys' home, a movement caught his eye. He strained to look more closely. There, not too far in the distance, near the gravesite he'd tidied that afternoon, stood a strange sight. It seemed to be the manifestation of a sailor in an old-fashioned uniform—except that it couldn't really be a sailor because the apparition before his eyes was transparent. Carson could clearly see through the image and out onto the Bay.

This encounter with the ghost was more than enough for George Carson. He told a reporter for the *Democrat and Chronicle* that he was "scared stiff" while he stood there watching the ghost pace between the Murphys' bench and the long-deceased sailor's burial plot. As Carson continued to watch, the image vanished before his eyes.

George Carson then hurried back to his own cabin. Even as he was doing so, he knew already that the first job he would tackle the next morning would be to reassemble the grave marker that he had so thoughtlessly cast aside the day before.

It would seem that this simple act of respect and acknowledgment was sufficient to calm the sailor's disturbed soul, for according to the newspaper article, after the stones were reassembled, the haunting stopped and life became "serene again on Point Charles."

Of course, that report was made on May 12, 1921, and there have been plenty of opportunities for ghostly activity on or near Sodus Bay since then. Maybe the *Democrat and Chronicle*, or any other newspaper, just hasn't seen fit to keep us up to date on more recently ghostly challenges to "serene" Point Charles on Sodus Bay.

Old Souls

According to legend, you'd be hard pressed to find a single naval installation more haunted than the United States Naval Shipyard in Norfolk, Virginia. Given the local history and ghosts' tendencies to become attached to physical materials, there's not much question as to why there are restless spirits around the place.

By the 1760s, Norfolk had become a busy port. Supplies, money and materials were not readily available, so when authorities began to construct the first expansion buildings on the surrounding land, they used the materials most readily at hand—discarded timber from sailing vessels that were no longer serviceable. This is probably

The pier at the Norfolk Naval Shipyard, around 1909; the site is notoriously haunted.

how the shipyard became haunted by a ghost dressed in garb from the days of the Revolutionary War.

People working around those haunted buildings have named the ghost "John Paul" because he resembles Revolutionary War hero John Paul Jones. The apparition is so clear that a World War II soldier actually broke his leg fleeing in fright from the harmless but lifelike image. The legacy of John Paul, the ghost, no doubt dates back to the original colonies' fight for freedom. Perhaps that legacy from the Revolutionary War continues to reverberate, or haunt, to the present day.

Second-Story Haunting

Occasionally, or perhaps frequently, ghostly energy seems to become absorbed by physical objects. Used bookstores, for instance, are often haunted. It is a widely accepted theory that supernatural energy imbued in the physical properties of the books has come into the store. The following tale is a nautical example of that phenomenon.

There was a building on a dock in Salem, Massachusetts, with an especially odd architectural style. The second story of the wooden structure always gave visitors the impression of being on board a ship. And there was a good reason for this. When the structure was built, the owner, a man named Herbert Miller, retrieved the hull of an abandoned sailing vessel and hoisted it on top of his recently constructed small shack. In that one maneuver, the man had gained a two-story dwelling—and a haunted one at that.

Author Robert Ellis Cahill toured the unusual building with a friend of his who was considering investing in the property and converting it into a restaurant. As Cahill inspected the place, he came to the part of the second floor that was once the stern of the resurrected vessel.

"Get out of here," a disembodied voice growled at him. Cahill wrote that he looked around him and saw that there was no one nearby. Just as he was beginning to doubt his own sanity and also settle back into looking around the place, he heard the voice again. "Get out of here," it repeated.

That second command was more than enough to convince Robert Ellis Cahill to leave the building immediately. It seemed that ghostly energy had been absorbed into some portions of that ship's hull that had formed the second story of the building. As a result, his friend never did open a restaurant in that building, even though he'd been so enthusiastic about the plan before.

Dear Molly Machay

James and Harold were just youngsters during that sweltering hot English summer in 1921. They spent most of their days trying to escape the terrible heat and humidity that blanketed the community where they lived. Fortunately, as this also meant escaping from the confines of their parents' watchful eyes, the boys were more than pleased with the arrangement.

Usually, they would hike or ride double on Harold's bicycle until they reached the beach just a few miles from town. On one particular day, they decided to trek farther. They hiked along the seaside until they came to a deserted little bay. Neither boy had ever been there before and they were both thoroughly intrigued with this new place to explore.

Harold took off his shoes and socks, rolled up his pants and waded into the cool, knee-deep water. As he walked, he disturbed hundreds of tiny fish that had been resting around the rocks in the bay. Startled, they swam frantically about, tickling the boy's ankles with their wet, scaly little bodies. The boy laughed at the strange sensation and called out to James.

"Come wading! There's more fish here than I've ever seen before in one place!"

James may have been the braver of the two friends, for he replied, "Wading? I'm going for a swim on the other side of those rocks!"

Stripping off his clothes down to his shorts, James lost no time in jumping into the cool water. He swam for some distance under water with his eyes tightly closed against the sting of the brine. As he came up for a breath, the boy gave a whoop of delight.

"That felt great!" James called out to Harold as he wiped the salty water from his face. Once he was sure no drops of water would get into his eyes, he opened them and looked around. And then he screamed. He screamed more loudly than he would've thought possible. The water directly before him was moving. Seconds later, a figure broke through the surface. It was a girl. Her hair was matted, her clothes torn, her skin as white as paper. She rose from the water as though being pushed up from a platform below, but when she reached what must have been her natural height, the horrid-looking vision didn't stop. Staring beseechingly at James, with arms held out to him, the dreadful manifestation continued to rise until, impossibly, she was well above the water.

"Let's get out of here," James screamed as he fled from the water, grabbing his clothes as he hit the rocky shore.

Harold looked puzzled—but just for a second, because that was when he saw the look on his friend's face and he knew something was very wrong. "What's wrong, James? You look as though you've seen a ghost."

"Shut up!" was the only reply he got.

The two lads ran as fast as their bare feet would take them until they had put several miles between themselves and the secluded bay. Even then, it was only exhaustion that finally slowed their pace.

"Let's go in there," James panted, pointing to a small store up the road. "We can get an icy and sit and rest."

The two pushed open the store's squeaky wooden screen door and entered the welcome, cool darkness of the roadside shop. They picked their frozen snacks from the icebox and, before starting to lick at the treats, brushed away the insulating sawdust from the frozen edges.

Harold, still dripping salt water, laid a two-penny coin on the counter and thanked the store owner.

"You boys look as though you need to sit and rest for a while. Have you had an adventure?" the man asked.

At first neither boy said a thing but even their silence told the shopkeeper everything he needed to know.

"You tried to swim in the bay, didn't you?" the older man asked.

James and Harold nodded mutely.

The man continued. "I'm betting then that you saw Molly. Dear Molly Machay. She drowned some years ago in that quiet little inlet. Her body's buried in the grave-yard out behind the store, but her spirit's never rested. They say that whenever a child tries to swim in the spot where she drowned, Molly's ghost rises up to warn the youngster that it's not safe."

James and Harold lost even more color from their faces as they listened to the man.

"That was a ghost?" Harold asked at exactly the same moment that James mumbled, "I saw a ghost?"

The old man nodded and smiled. "You sure did. You saw the ghost of Molly Machay. She was a classmate of mine when we were kids. It was more than 50 years ago now that the poor thing drowned. She didn't mean to frighten you. She just wanted to warn you. She didn't want you to die like she did."

Speechless, James and Harold nodded their good-byes to the shopkeeper and headed out the door. Every summer's day after that one, the boys spent their time at the beach nearest their homes. They never again went back to the bay where they'd seen Molly's ghost. Still, though, for years afterward, they referred to the summer of 1921 as their haunted summer.

The Lost Villages

A ghost town is an inherently spooky sight. Seeing all those empty buildings and roads devoid of any traffic, where lives once thrived, has a predictable emotional impact on a person visiting the place. Of course, the fact that most ghost towns are haunted by the ghosts of those who once lived in the now-deserted towns only serves to enhance that eerie ambience.

The only site spookier than that of a ghost town would have to be a *submerged* ghost town—an abandoned community lying under tons and tons of seawater. And, strangely enough, that is exactly what can be found at the bottom of the St. Lawrence Seaway between the cities of

Cornwall and Kingston in the Canadian province of Ontario. Stranger still is that there's more than just *one* drowned community on the floor of the Seaway—there are half a dozen of them.

The St. Lawrence Seaway was created to improve shipping access along the St. Lawrence River by widening and deepening the bed. Years of intensive work were required to create the seaway and to move everything, including people, out of the towns. Finally "Inundation Day" arrived on July 1, 1958, which also happened to be Dominion Day, the annual national holiday now known as Canada Day. More than 25,000 people gathered to watch an explosion destroy the last dam, thus releasing a torrential wave of water. The flood surged and the waters buried the once snug villages forever. The land on which some of the battles of the War of 1812 had been fought was now submerged.

Some people responded with jubilation. The citizens of Cornwall, for instance, marked the occasion with parades and celebrations. To those folks, the seaway meant a prosperous future. Other people, mostly those who had called the drowned towns home, mourned the loss that occurred that day. Many of those folk continued to mourn their bizarre and devastating loss until the day they died.

Author Rosemary Rutley's book, *Voices from the Lost Villages,* includes many firsthand accounts from people who lived through that unique and daring removal and resettlement project. Even 40 years after the traumatic event, the people she interviewed, whose lives had been devastated by the watery change, still felt the loss.

Donald Stuart was 30 years old when Inundation Day buried the town where he'd been born and where his family had lived for two centuries. In the late 1990s, his sorrow was still evident. "I hated it," he flatly declared. "I hated it like hell."

Because Stuart's ancestors had long rested in peace under the land they'd lived on, their graves, and those of more than 5000 others, were disinterred and relocated to two new towns that had been built to house the living who were displaced. Other survivors did not want their relatives' graves disturbed. Thier bodies are now buried under not only several feet of earth, but also under the millions of gallons of water covering that earth.

All of this disruption has unquestionably made modern, efficient shipping possible along what used to be a waterway dotted with rapids, shallow sections and intruding shorelines and has had economic benefits. An unintended result has been the creation of a haven for SCUBA divers. With air tanks strapped to their backs and flippers on their feet, divers can easily swim in and around the buildings that, for one reason or another, were left on their original sites. The swimmers can even explore the remaining gravesites. Not surprisingly, these underwater explorers have occasionally reported being startled by a sudden inexplicable sensation. They got the feeling that they were not alone—even though they knew that, aside from their diving companions, they should be absolutely alone. Divers today continue to report similar experiences.

Some divers have also seen strange shapes moving about in and around those lost villages. Sailors have seen lights shining weakly from below the water's black surface. They have also been frightened when disembodied and indistinct voices have been heard coming from locations directly above where the towns lie in their watery graves. It seems that at least some former residents of those beloved little communities don't realize that their hometowns are now buried below the Seaway. The deceased, or rather the ghosts of the deceased, continue to go about their daily lives, apparently unaware that they are haunting submerged ghost towns.

6
Mysterious
Areas

A re certain places on earth more prone to supernatural activity? The best answer to that question, so far at least, seems to be "Probably." After you read these stories, though, you might form a stronger opinion.

Terror-Filled Triangle

The Bermuda Triangle is a strange and dangerous place. We all know of at least a few tragic and inexplicable events that have occurred over the years within the three points surrounding this mysterious area. According to the American Naval Historical Center in Washington, D.C., the triangular area "is generally accepted to be Bermuda; Miami, Florida; and San Juan, Puerto Rico." Interestingly, this official and precise description is juxtaposed against the following further information: "The U.S. Board of Geographic Names does not recognize the Bermuda Triangle as an official name and does not maintain an official file on the area."

According to that same source, the Coast Guard takes a similar stance of skepticism and denial. Again, according to the Historical Center, "the Coast Guard is not impressed with supernatural explanations of disasters at sea. It has been their experience that the combined forces of nature and unpredictability of mankind outdo even the most far-fetched science fiction…"

Despite these assertions, there can be no denying that over the years, numerous ships and planes, along with all those aboard those vehicles, have apparently vanished within that triangular 440,000 square-mile (1,140,000 square-kilometer) portion of the Atlantic Ocean. This one area has perhaps more supernatural stories associated with it than any other area on earth. Dozens of excellent books, documentaries and even feature films have dealt with the mysteries of the Bermuda Triangle. In other words, the phenomenon has been skillfully and

Placid Caribbean waters near the Bermuda Triangle conceal a strange paranormal energy.

thoroughly covered. For our purposes here, we shall highlight only a few of the instances.

Early in March 1918, USS *Cyclops* set sail from Brazil. As she sailed into the area we now refer to as the Bermuda Triangle, this 20,000-ton ship and her crew—

vanished. Even the American Navy acknowledges that the *Cyclops'* demise has remained a mystery all these years. No trace of that ship, nor the sailors aboard her, has ever been discovered—nor has any possible cause for her disappearance ever been offered.

☠

On December 5, 1945, five planes, torpedo bomber aircraft under American Navy colors, left a military base at Fort Lauderdale, Florida. The planes' crews (a total of 14 men) were on a training mission. The bombers were well out over the sea, flying over the Bermuda Triangle, when the tower at Fort Lauderdale began receiving distress calls from the squadron. Moments later, those calls stopped. Absolutely nothing more is known about the fate of those aircraft or the men flying in them, but not because of lack of interest or effort.

A search and rescue party was immediately sent out in a seaplane to locate the missing planes and bring them safely back home. The rescue mission not only failed, but that plane and all of those on board her also vanished. No trace of any of the six planes or their occupants has ever been found. No clue has ever been unearthed to explain those seemingly impossible disappearances.

Similarly the fates of a DC-3 aircraft (carrying 27 souls) and a Globemaster (carrying 53 souls), in 1948 and 1951 respectively, are also completely unknown. In 1963, a tanker known as the *Marine Sulphur Queen* inexplicably vanished while sailing through the Bermuda Triangle. The

For nearly 100 years, the Bermuda Triangle has terrified sailors in the Caribbean.

disappearance of the ship, with all 39 hands on board, has never been solved.

Although some scientists may offer rationalizations for each of these enigmatic incidents, it still seems wiser to avoid testing the fates, or whatever is in control in that part of the Atlantic Ocean, by entering the strange space.

Underwater Monolith

On a fine summer-like day in the spring of 1804, Captain Charles Selleck aboard the *Lady Murray* was nearing the end of an uneventful voyage to Presqu'ile Point in the eastern end of Lake Ontario. The trip had gone every bit as well as Selleck had expected. Not only was the captain an experienced leader, but his crew was also capable, and the *Lady Murray* had always proven to be a reliable vessel. Selleck was surprised, therefore, when one of his sailors filed a very strange report. It seemed that something decidedly odd had been spotted in the water just ahead.

The captain accompanied the man topside and immediately saw exactly why the sailor had been so concerned. Selleck had sailed this route many times and knew that the water depth in the area was consistent. Even so, the waves over one small area were behaving as though the water was very shallow at that spot. The only other explanation for such wave movement was that something lay hidden just below the water's surface.

Whichever the case might be, to Captain Selleck's well-trained eye, a significant navigational hazard lay dead ahead. He ordered that the *Lady Murray* be stopped immediately and that a rowboat and crew be sent out to investigate this potentially threatening anomaly.

Less than an hour later, the sailors from the rowboat were back on the deck of the *Lady Murray*. The information they brought with them was virtually useless to Selleck because it made no sense. The men who'd rowed close to the area declared that a huge rock was just under the surface of the water. Of course, Captain Selleck knew

this could not be so. Not only had these waters been carefully charted, but he had also sailed over the area many
times before and had certainly never encountered any sort
of rock at any point in the trip.

Clearly, the captain would have to check this out for
himself. Unfortunately, his investigation did nothing to
ease his mind, for he could see that the situation was even
more threatening than he'd feared. As Selleck peered over
the edges of the small boat and into the water, he saw a
massive and solid object less than 3 feet (1 meter) beneath
the surface of the water.

The captain ordered soundings done to determine the
object's size. Perhaps if they knew how big this thing was,
they would have a clue as to what it could be. Much to
Selleck's frustration, the sounding tests only clouded the
mystery further. The results revealed that, whatever was in
front of their ship was about 40 feet (12 meters) square
and 300 feet (90 meters) tall!

Selleck knew that such a height was completely impossible. The lake was not that deep near Presqu'ile Bay.
Something must have gone wrong with the testing. He
ordered the tests repeated. The results of the new tests
were the same. Captain Selleck and the entire crew of the
Lady Murray were staring down at an enormous, solid
monolith that, impossibly, had not been there just days
before. This meant that what they were confirming visu-
ally, as well as with sound tests, could not possibly exist.

But it did.

Captain Selleck returned to the *Lady Murray*, replotted
a route to shore and then made for port as quickly as possible. Once there, he reported his findings to authorities

and asked that the area be marked as a serious navigational hazard.

Word of this astonishing find spread throughout the shipping community. Everyone wanted to see this strange anomaly for themselves. Aboard all sizes and shapes of craft, people flocked to the spot in the lake where the *Lady Murray* had discovered the enormous submerged column. Soon after, attempting to knock the slab down became a sport. Despite the best efforts of many folk, no one succeeded in even denting the object of their curiosities.

One person who came out to inspect the tombstone-like structure was government employee Captain Thomas Paxton. Charles Selleck himself took Paxton out to the site because Paxton was one of the masters of the *Speedy*, a government-owned ship, and therefore had an interest in navigational hazards.

As Paxton and Selleck inspected the unknown submerged structure, the *Speedy* was in Toronto harbor waiting for her scheduled Sunday departure to points east on Lake Ontario. She would be carrying an odd assortment of passengers—government officials, court officials, a prisoner on his way to be hanged, as well as others who wanted to make the trip.

Captain James Richardson was scheduled to command the *Speedy* on that voyage, but as the day of departure drew closer, he became uncomfortable about the upcoming sailing. He tried in vain to get the trip cancelled or at least postponed. Although he was an experienced Great Lakes captain, he had a premonition of doom so strong that it overrode his usual sense of responsibility. In the end, Captain Richardson refused to go on the trip.

Thomas Paxton was called upon to fill in.

Had Richardson's superiors listened to the warnings he tried to give them about the certain dangers he felt were ahead, history could have been very different.

Some of the passengers booked to sail on the *Speedy* that day must have shared Richardson's sense of foreboding, for many of them cancelled their reservations and took other modes of transportation to their destinations. Despite these changes, however, the *Speedy*, its crew and remaining passengers departed as scheduled.

Not far from her home port, the *Speedy* encountered a severe storm. People on the shoreline reported that the bad weather seemed to follow the struggling ship. The witnesses were shocked that the captain did not make any attempt to escape such threatening weather by heading back to shore. Those on the shore could see that, if something wasn't done, tragedy was imminent. They built bonfires as markers to help the captain bring the ship safely into a temporary harbor.

Their efforts were ignored. Witnesses even went so far as to imply that it seemed as though the ship was no longer under the captain's control. The doomed vessel sailed directly to the area where Selleck and the *Lady Murray* had discovered the submerged monolith. And, just as the *Speedy* approached that potentially lethal spot below, the weather became even more severe.

The terrible storm closed in around the floundering ship. The *Speedy* was never seen again.

As soon as it was safe to do so, a search was organized. No trace of the *Speedy* was ever found. Soon officials abandoned hope of finding any survivors, but in an effort to clear up the mystery of the ship's disappearance, they decided to drag the lake in the area where witnesses reported losing sight of the missing ship. Wary of the monolith and the hazards it posed, the searchers cast their nets.

Not only did they not find any wreckage, but the submerged column was also gone. The enormous structure that had appeared so suddenly had just as suddenly and just a mysteriously disappeared. If the power of the storm or the force of the *Speedy* possibly crashing into it had toppled the edifice, then there should at least have been a pile of rubble on the lake floor.

But there was nothing.

The monolith, the ship and all aboard it vanished without a trace during a November storm in 1804.

Buried Boat

The following quirky story is a contradiction to the vanishing ships' stories, for this time a ship was found— a ship for which no identity could be established.

It was 1922, and the Roaring Twenties were in full force. The world economy was booming. Everyone *had* more and was *doing* more.

A cottage owner on the St. Lawrence River decided to build a dock on his property. He hired a crew of men to dig holes for pilings on which to set the platform. As the men dug, they routinely hit rocks and cast them aside.

When their shovels hit on a completely flat surface, they were puzzled and took some time to expose a bit more of the buried mass. Once the workers realized that they had come across a man-made object, they called the homeowner to come to take a look. Curious as to what it could be, the man had the crew clear away more earth.

There, buried roughly 6 feet (1.8 meters) down, was an almost perfectly preserved lake-going vessel.

Careful examination revealed that there had once been a fire aboard this craft, but it had been contained to one area of the ship's cabin. Tools were also unearthed. The type of vessel and the style of its construction led those assessing the strange situation to conclude that the long-buried boat had been built about a century and a half before the workers unearthed it. Despite efforts made to trace its identity, no one was ever able to explain the strange nautical find.

Message in a Bottle

For nearly a century, the story of the *Picton*'s disappearance was one of the most puzzling from that same mysterious region. The *Picton* and her two sister ships, the *Minnes* and the *Acacia*, were making their way toward the eastern end of Lake Ontario. The three sailed along within view of one another on a clear June day. Then, without any warning whatsoever, the *Picton* vanished from sight. One moment she was there and the next she was gone without a trace. It was as if she had suddenly sailed into another dimension.

Because the disappearance had been witnessed by the crews of two other ships, the search for the *Picton* began immediately. Despite both their promptness and experience on these waters, their search went unrewarded.

Word spread to the shore, and those in nearby ports kept watch for any sign of the missing ship. At first nothing was found, then days later something bobbing in the water caught a young boy's attention. He rowed out to the object and brought it back to shore. It was a securely sealed bottle with a handwritten note inside—a note written by the captain of the *Picton*.

The message revealed that the captain knew he had only moments to live. How then had he been able to write and insert this message into the bottle, especially as the captains of both the *Minnes* and the *Acacia* had reported the *Picton*'s disappearance had been absolutely instantaneous?

Other than that final, enigmatic note from the ship's captain, no trace of the ship has ever been found.

"Odd Attraction"

Nearly 80 years later and somewhat to the east of where the *Speedy* vanished, a coal-carrying ship named the *Quinlan* also went missing. It was scheduled to sail directly through the Marysburg Vortex, an area of Lake Ontario that some people feel shares characteristics with the Bermuda Triangle. There are similarities in the two ships' disappearances that cannot be overlooked, but in the case of the *Quinlan*, there were survivors, so we have been left with firsthand accounts of the bizarre episode.

Not long after the *Quinlan* left port at Oswego in New York, a dense blanket of fog closed around it. As the craft journeyed, shrouded from view, the temperature dropped dramatically around the craft, and a highly localized storm struck. Snow began to fall so heavily that every available hand was assigned to shovel the decks to prevent the ship from becoming top heavy and capsizing. Despite their best efforts, the sailors were unable to keep up. The snow was falling faster than they could shovel it away, and it was accumulating at a dangerous and frightening rate.

Strong winds blew up and enormous waves began to buffet the ship about, making it unsafe for anyone to stay on deck. It was all the men could do to just hang on for their lives. The captain was equally powerless. The force of the storm was in charge and it was threatening the very structure of the ship under his command.

The ship's compass had ceased to function. Even without that instrument, though, the captain knew that the severe storm had thrown him well off course and also that his men were exhausted and terrified. Unfortunately, these were no longer even remotely important issues in this perilous situation, for the ship's leader also knew that he had lost control of his own ship. The strange storm, or whatever had caused it, had completely taken over command of the *Quinlan*.

Eventually the badly damaged ship was tossed near the shore where rescuers waited to offer assistance. Only a few lives were saved. Even as the men on the shore reached out to grasp the sailors, the force of the gale, combined with the intense water and air pressure created as the *Quinlan* sank, took all but a few of those on board to their watery graves.

Once the survivors had been taken to safety and warmth in nearby homes, the full story began to unfold. All those who lived to tell of the deadly encounter agreed that the captain of the *Quinlan* had not been in control of the foundering ship. These experienced sailors, relieved to have escaped with their lives, unanimously stated that their lost ship had been "gripped by some odd attraction."

It has never been determined what that "odd attraction" might have been. The eastern end of Lake Ontario is known to possess areas of magnetic anomalies and isolated fogs, but none of these would have explained such an encounter, for this freak storm actually appeared to pursue the *Quinlan* before overtaking and sinking it.

No scientific explanation has ever been offered for this dreadful tragedy. The only explanations ever proposed were paranormal in nature. The ship had been another victim of an unknown force—a force that is perhaps not from our world.

English Enigma

Perhaps an equally mysterious force, similar to that said to exist in the infamous Bermuda Triangle, is responsible for the following true story reported by an English pilot.

In October 1978, pilot Malcolm Montgomerie, his copilot Adrian Purdy and Montgomerie's teenaged daughter Alison flew out of an airstrip near England's southwest coast. They were heading toward the Channel Islands for a weekend's getaway. At first all indications were that this would be a routine flight. And it should have been, for Montgomerie and Purdy were experienced pilots who had made this trip many times.

Just as they were approaching the Channel, instruments in the plane's cockpit began spinning wildly as though being manipulated by a strange magnetic field. Both the direction indicator and the compass needle darted first to the left and then to the right—at least 100 degrees in each direction. The only way Montgomerie could keep his bearings was by using his radio direction finder.

This life-threatening anomaly lasted for an agonizing 12 minutes. After that, the instruments stabilized as suddenly as they had gone out of control, and the group landed safely at their intended destination.

After spending two peaceful days enjoying life on the Channel Islands, the group boarded the plane once again—this time to head home. Thinking that their strange and frightening experience on their trip out was just a freak occurrence, they were not much concerned about the flight home. Unfortunately for Purdy and the two Montgomeries, their optimism was not well-placed.

At exactly the same point, the plane's instruments once again went berserk. This time whatever force was causing this dangerous situation remained with them for only five minutes, but by the time they flew out of its control, they were 20 miles off course.

Montgomerie reported his encounters to the Civil Aviation Authority, which issued a warning to pilots that such phenomena could occur at that particular area. A few days after that warning was released, however, the Defense Ministry declared, "We know of nothing that might have caused this."

Perhaps that official attitude explains why we have not had many other reports of unexplained occurrences over the English Channel.

Great Lakes

Legends of ships disappearing on the Great Lakes go back hundreds of years. Many of those disappearances, however, are not as mysterious as it would first appear.

The *Edmund Fitzgerald*, for instance, vanished from sight during one of the "storms of November" in 1975. For years there was speculation about what might have happened to that freighter especially as another ship, the *Anderson*, was traveling within sight of the *Fitz*. The captains of the two ships were keeping a special watch out for one another. Captain Cooper of the *Anderson* declared that he had looked up and had seen the *Edmund Fitzgerald*, then looked down at his instruments. When he looked up again just a few minutes later, the ship was nowhere to be seen. How could anything as big as a ship possibly disappear so quickly?

It was years before the remains of the *Fitz* was found, but when it was, investigators knew they did not have much of a mystery on their hands. The ship had been carrying tons of salt. The heavy snows had soaked the salt, increasing its weight to more than the ship could hold. She broke in two and plunged to the bottom of Lake Superior.

The gales of November were likely also responsible for the "disappearances" of the *Regina*, the *James C. Carruthers* and the *Charles Price*. All three enormous ships were lost, sunk no doubt, during a storm in November 1913.

But in November 1952, at a point almost directly above the spot where the *Fitzgerald* would sink in 1975, a privately owned plane, a Beech 35 aircraft, really did disappear. The pilot, a man whose name is recorded on Department of Transport documents as F. Jake, and his three passengers were heading for Toronto.

Both American and Canadian flight controllers had been in communication with Jake and had him on their radar—until the dot on those screens that represented the small Beech 35 flickered off. To date, no sign of the plane or any of its occupants has been seen. This disappearance has even been officially recognized. The Canadian government's report indicates, in part, that "despite an extensive search, no trace of the aircraft or occupants was found." The report concluded by acknowledging that "for undetermined reasons, [the plane] disappeared in Lake Superior."

The following year a US-Airforce F-86 jet interceptor flying over the same position in the lake also disappeared.

Reporters seized on the story immediately, and the *Chicago Tribune* printed the story under the headline "Jet, Two Aboard, Vanished Over Lake Superior." The reporter had even captured an official quotation from the United States Air Force: "The plane was followed on radar until it merged with an object 70 miles off Keweenaw Point in Upper Michigan. No trace was found of the airmen or the jet…"

Before many copies of that day's newspaper hit the streets, the Air Force squelched the story, and little more was heard about the incident. Rumors circulated for years that the "object" the jet merged with was a UFO. Interestingly, the plane disappeared at almost exactly the same spot where the ship the *Bannockburn* disappeared on November 18, 1902.

☠

On Thursday, May 21, 1959, a Piper seaplane, towing a canoe from its pontoons, disappeared with three people on board, once again, over Lake Superior. Only the canoe was ever found.

In this case there is also an official statement documenting the disappearance, only this report has an interesting twist. As the statement indicated, "An extensive search of the lake was made by dragging underwater detection equipment, divers, a deep sea bell and sonar equipment. Several sweeps were also made with airborne detection equipment."

None of the above is extraordinary for a government report about such an incident. The next statement, however, is very unusual for such an account: "Grappling hooks engaged an object where detection gear had given a strong reading, but all efforts to bring the object to the surface failed. The object engaged was in 320 feet [96 meters] of water. A diver descended to 250 feet [75 meters], but due to darkness under water could not make any visual contact. The sonar gear established that the lake bottom was very uneven, with deep holes, the deepest being 590 feet [177 meters]."

All fruitless efforts, with their puzzling results, were discontinued. Neither the plane nor any of its passengers have ever been seen again.

☠

Many other planes have disappeared while flying over the Great Lakes: a CF-101 Canadian Air Force interceptor vanished on September 27, 1960. A twin turbo jet Lear aircraft went missing over Lake Michigan on November 6, 1969. No trace of the plane or its occupants has ever been found.

On December 16, 1959, the pilot of a small plane radioed the airport at Windsor, Ontario, to advise that he would be landing shortly. The plane never made it, but its ruins were found the next week floating on Lake St. Clair (between Lake Erie and Lake Huron). The wreck was deemed by authorities to have been "liveable," and those aboard may actually have survived the crash. We'll never know, though, because despite an expensive and thorough search of the lake, no bodies were ever found.

These disappearances are both tragic and thought provoking at the same time. When you couple them with reports that Jacques Cartier and Samuel de Champlain took back to France, you have even more of an enigma. These two explorers had been told at length about the legend that there were once "shining cities of light" where "men who fly like birds" lived on the shores of the Great Lakes. Could the story have been just a fanciful tale, or was it proof of an otherworldly encounter?

☠

Keeping that ancient legend in mind makes the following story even more intriguing.

During the evening of April 28, 1937, Captain George Donner, skipper of the ship *O.M. McFarland*, went to his cabin for a short nap. His plan seemed logical, as the lake was calm and the trip had been absolutely uneventful.

Donner had asked to be awakened as the *McFarland* approached her destination of Port Washington on Lake Erie. Three hours later, almost to the minute, the ship's second mate knocked on the door of the captain's cabin. There was no reply. He knocked again. And again and again. Finally, the man slowly eased the door open. He didn't know what to expect, but he certainly expected to find something—but he didn't. Donner was not in his cabin.

In a panic, the sailor organized a search party. The searchers scoured every inch of the ship but could not find their leader. There was nothing to do but dock the craft and report the man's disappearance.

Some on shore initially suggested that Donner had gone overboard—either on purpose or by accident, but further inquiries deemed that this was highly unlikely.

The captain had many years of experience, and the seas were calm. It would not have been possible for him to have accidentally been washed into the lake. And suicide was completely beyond reason, for the man's life was in good order and he took great pleasure and satisfaction from it.

For weeks after the loss, ships sailing along that navigational route were asked to keep a special watch out for any sign of Captain Donner's body or any indication at all that he had drowned. None was ever found. The mystery of the man's disappearance remains completely unsolved. No clues have ever been found. Was this perhaps the result of a "close encounter" with an inexplicable force? We can only speculate.

7

Phantom
Ships

A phantom ship is an image of a vessel still plying the world's waterways, even though the physical ship has already gone to its watery afterlife. This paranormal phenomenon is more common than you might expect and very frightening for those who experience it. Each floating apparition is routinely referred to as a "Flying Dutchman" in reference to the first recorded ghost or phantom ship.

Infamous Omen

Ghost lore has it that the original *Flying Dutchman* may have sailed the seas around Africa's Cape of Good Hope sometime in the 1200s. Many versions of the legend still persist. Another tale suggests that the *Flying Dutchman* sailed several centuries later. That ship's captain murdered both his wife and his brother. He was then allegedly driven mad from guilt and regret and died completely insane, his tortured soul doomed to sail forever, never reaching port. A variation on that tale has the captain working his crew far too hard. When he made a last, life-threatening decision during a journey, the men mutinied, killed the captain and threw him overboard. His angry soul apparently sails on into a condemned eternity.

With such a terrible history, it is not surprising that seeing a legendary phantom ship, a *Flying Dutchman*, is believed by sailors all over the world to be a bad omen. Such a sighting, they are convinced, foreshadows very bad luck aboard their ship.

Perhaps the most famous sighting of a *Flying Dutchman* occurred on board the British ship H.M.S. *Inconstant* during the evening of July 11, 1881. The mirage was duly noted in the ship's log as it properly should have been, but that was not what made this occasion so notable. It was the fact that one of the sailors was a prince—the man who would become King George V, ruler of Britain and all her holdings.

Despite the fact that acknowledging the ghost might have damaged his reputation, this member of the royal family thereafter always noted that the ship's records were indeed correct. Those aboard and awake at 4:00 that

The lore surrounding the Flying Dutchman *reflects the mysterious nature of the sea.*

morning all supported their captain's eerily detailed, two-sentence report.

"The *Flying Dutchman* crossed our bow. She emitted a strange phosphorescent light as of a phantom ship all aglow, in the midst of which light the masts, spars and sails of a brig 200 yards [180 meters] distant stood out in strong relief as she came up on the port bow where also the officer of the watch from the bridge saw her, as did also the quarter-deck midshipman, who was sent forward at once to the forecastle, but on arriving there was no vestige nor any sign whatever of any material ship to be seen either near or right away to the horizon, the night being clear and the sea calm."

Although the ghost ship had been seen for centuries before that summer's night, the veracity of the phenomenon was really underlined by its royal acknowledgment. It did not, of course, explain how such an apparition of a ship could possibly exist. After all, if the ghost of a person is a spectral remnant of the person's soul, then what, on this earthly plane or on others, could a ghost ship be? Surely ships, or for that matter any object made by humans, cannot have a soul.

Still, in certain cases—sailing vessels certainly being one of those—physical objects apparently become imbued with the essence of life as a result of the intense emotions people connected with them feel. The strength of emotions causes these vessels that have been gone for so many years to appear on the world's seas. Of course, no one understands the powers that cause encounters between the two planes. Does the phantom exist because of the person witnessing it or do the astonished witnesses see the phantom because it does exist for them to see? We cannot know for certain. We do know that some of the best ghost stories of the sea involve a sighting of a *Flying Dutchman*. Some even include the ghosts of sailors aboard their ghostly ship!

Riverboat Wraith

People in boats along the Missouri River, near Jefferson City, Missouri, occasionally see a unique steamboat making its way up that wide river. She is propelled by a paddle system that has not been used for over 100 years. Despite this anomaly, she glides along her route carrying a crew and about a dozen passengers, all of whom seem to be enjoying themselves.

But she is a ghost ship. The boat's recognizable propulsion system is not the only clue that this is not a vessel from our plane. A closer inspection of the image reveals that the paddle wheeler hovers a few feet above the surface of the water.

Sorrowful Sarah

Sarah was usually seen through later afternoon mists and only ever at Hopewell Harbor in Maine on America's east coast. Her story is sad. This phantom ship was named for Sarah Soule, the love of the shipbuilder's life. Another man, Charles Jose, also loved Miss Soule, and in 1812, a battle between the two men ensued. Jose was killed, but some of his associates lashed the shipbuilder to the mast of his vessel, the *Sarah*, and then cast the ship adrift.

Eventually, some citizens of Hopewell Harbor sailed out to the *Sarah* and rescued the trapped man from his foundering ship. He was then reunited with his love. The ship could not be saved and it sank not long after Sarah's love had been returned to land. For years, however, the ghost ship was seen in Hopewell Harbor just before afternoon turned into evening. By now, the *Sarah* may have gone to her eternal dry dock because the last recorded sighting of her ghost was made in 1880.

Phantom Ship Snippets

Perhaps because the story of the original *Flying Dutchman* is more than 700 years old, one could assume that all phantoms of the sea are ancient sailing ships, those that have long ago left the waterways on *this* side of time's curtain. More modern vessels have also been encountered. Somewhere atop the murky depths of the Atlantic Ocean, for instance, sailors have reported seeing a World War II destroyer make its way toward them.

Some phantom ships, such as the Khosou, *are heard, not seen.*

The phantom ship is so clear that, when it's first seen, the witness presumes that it is an actual battleship, but soon it becomes evident that there is nothing and no one alive aboard the vessel. As awestruck sailors watch in silent terror the image then vanishes from view—as mysteriously and quickly as it had appeared.

Heard but Not Seen

Occasionally, a phantom ship will be heard but not seen. Such a supernatural encounter is apparently also extremely distressing.

The crew aboard the *Khosou* experienced this phenomenon as they were making their way from Bombay to Calcutta on the Indian Ocean. Weather had closed in. The fog surrounding their ship was as dense as any aboard could remember having seen. The craft's captain ordered that the speed be reduced to bare movement and that the *Khosou*'s foghorn be sounded every two minutes.

Seconds after the first bleat from the horn trumpeted out into the misty atmosphere, those aboard the *Khosou* were startled to hear another ship's foghorn reply to theirs. The sailors knew this instant response meant that their ship was dangerously close to another. In order to avert a collision, the crew shut down all the *Khosou*'s engines. The ship remained stationary for the next few hours, not daring to move while blinded by such fog and in close proximity to an unknown vessel. As a courtesy, the sailors aboard each of the stranded ships continued to sound their foghorn signals.

Hours later, when the fog lifted, the ghostly sounding echoes of warning signals ended. The seas around the *Khosou* were utterly calm—and equally empty. Not one sign that another ship was nearby, or even had ever been nearby, existed.

It wasn't until sometime later that the captain finally discovered the truth about that eerie encounter. On January 5, 1931, the *Tricoleur*, a freighter carrying a cargo of chemicals, had exploded at sea. The blast sunk the ship—at exactly the spot where the *Khosou* had, that frightening day, been forced to wait out the weather.

Great Lakes Ghosts

Many boats of all sizes and shapes have disappeared while on various voyages across the Great Lakes of North America. Some of those vessels, such as the *Edmund Fitzgerald*, are eventually found resting on the lake bed, but others are never seen again—except as specters plying the waters. The *L.R. Doty* disappeared in 1898, shortly after it left Chicago, Illinois, bound for Midland, Ontario. Neither the ship nor any of her crew were ever seen again—except as ghosts upon Lake Michigan.

In 1901, the *Nashua* and those aboard her met a similar fate on Lake Huron. They too sail on into eternity, apparently oblivious to the knowledge that, in this world, they no longer exist.

The following year the *Celtic* had nearly completed a relatively short trip on Lake Huron when she disappeared. For years afterward, her image was seen scuttling just ahead of other ships, crewed by sailors whose eyes were held to the wraith in terror-filled fascination.

Square Rigger

In 2001, a retired merchant marine sailor named Jay Green gave a decidedly strange report. It seems that in 1949, he was on a ship bound from Honolulu to San Francisco. At one point, as he kept watch during the voyage, a strange illusion sailed before his eyes. He explained that it looked to be a "square rigger" and the old ship "looked real enough" although they knew even as they were watching her that the old craft was an illusion because, of course, no vessels like that had sailed the waterways of this world for many, many years.

Afterlife Saver

The name of one of the ships involved in this ghostly encounter was reported as the steamship Mallory Knight; *however, there is reason to believe that this may be a pseudonym used for security purposes. The following events occurred during the days just after peace had been declared in 1945.*

"Good morning, sir. My name's Earl Sheffield, retired Royal Navy captain. It would seem as though you and I will be sharing this compartment in the train for the balance of our trip," the dignified middle-aged man said as he entered the small, semi-private cabin on the express train from Brighton to London, England.

"Pleased to make your acquaintance," a younger man, who was already settled into one of the well-padded benches, responded. "My name is Matthew and, by coincidence, I, too, have a connection with the Navy. I'm sure we will have a great deal to talk about."

"And what specifically is your connection with sailing? Have you been in the service, then?" Sheffield inquired as he settled into the train's plush compartment.

"No, as a matter of fact, I haven't," Matthew answered. "I work in banking, but my father was a Navy man. He was the skipper of the *Regent Panther*, which..."

"The *Regent Panther*?" the older man interrupted. "My word son, that *is* a coincidence. Let me tell you about my experience with your father's ship. I wonder if he'd ever have told you about this incident. Possibly not as it was surely considerably more important to me than it was to him. And, it's certainly a story well worth relating."

Retired Captain Sheffield immediately launched into his tale of the encounter with the *Regent Panther*. His recitation took up almost every second of the train trip.

According to the man's retelling, the *Mallory Knight*, with Sheffield himself at the helm, was headed, without an escort, through a particularly dangerous area of the South Pacific Ocean. It was during the autumn of 1943, and World War II was at its height. Although sailing unescorted was unusual, this current voyage for the *Mallory Knight* involved an important and highly secret mission. Therefore, the risk of sailing solo was warranted. Sheffield's ship was headed to South Point on Guimara Island in the Philippines to deliver sophisticated electronics equipment for the war effort.

The voyage had been without incident. But as they were about to sail through the treacherous Guimara Straits, Sheffield knew that it would take equal amounts of skill, daring and luck to successfully navigate the strait— especially as their charts for that area were missing. Captain Sheffield knew he was up against a difficult and important test of his abilities as a leader of seamen.

Stern-faced and at the wheel, the man began barking "slow ahead" orders. Moments later his second mate came running into the wheelhouse, calling out to the captain, "I have information that we need, sir, the information that would have been on those missing charts. A ship from just beyond South Point flashed the coordinates to our signalman of the most serious hazards. I have them here."

The captain's face showed the relief he felt, but he tried not to acknowledge his feelings for fear of revealing how dreadfully concerned he had been. "Acknowledge the message and ask the other vessel to identify herself," Sheffield told the man.

The second mate nodded and quickly left the wheelhouse, leaving Sheffield to give orders and to see that they were followed accurately.

Later that day in the officer's mess, the men were eating their supper and reviewing the day's events when the captain thought to ask the second mate if the ship that had relayed the important information to them had identified herself to the *Mallory*'s communications' crew.

"Yes," the other man replied. "Apparently she was the *Regent Panther* whose home port is Liverpool."

Back on the train chugging its way into London, Captain Sheffield turned to Matthew, his temporary companion, and said, "It must have been your father's ship that saved mine from running aground on shoals. Without the intervention from the crew under your father's command we would not have been able to deliver the communications gear for the battles in the South Pacific. Isn't it amazing that today, in peacetime, you and I should end up sharing this bunk?"

Matthew was silent for several moments while he gathered his thoughts. When he replied to Sheffield, he spoke very slowly and quietly.

"More amazing still, sir, is that it wasn't actually my father's ship that saved your mission. That could not have been my father's ship. It must have been the ghost of my father's ship—a *Flying Dutchman*. You see, sir, the *Regent Panther* sank, taking all hands, including my father, with it. That happened in 1923—more than 20 years before."

And so, although seeing a *Flying Dutchman* usually portends tragedy, seeing the signals made by a phantom ship obviously brought the *Mallory Knight* life-sparing good fortune.

"A Biscuit Toss Away"

Silence, stillness and darkness; that was all there was for the crew aboard the *Annie M. Reid* that night. Captain Durkee ordered the anchor lowered and the sails furled while they waited for dawn. An uneasy atmosphere permeated the very air those sailors breathed. No one spoke. Everyone knew that rounding the Cape of Good Hope could be wrought with difficulty and danger. To be stranded by such complete calm at that place, a point they were eager to pass by quickly, was definitely not reassuring to the men. All they could do was wait out the calm sea and their own anxieties as best they could.

After his senses had become used to the deafening silence, the blinding darkness and the eerie stillness, Captain Durkee thought he heard and saw and felt changes occurring around him. He reacted with an involuntary shudder. *Is my mind playing tricks on me?* he wondered. But Durkee was a well-experienced man of the sea and not about to let his currently unnerved imagination govern the safety of the *Annie M. Reid* and all aboard her. He picked up his spyglass and tried to peer out over the inky black world around him.

What is that over there? he wondered as he watched an unidentifiable disturbance roil about on the water just 50 feet (15 meters) from his ship.

Seconds later he felt a cold breeze swirl about him. The strange disturbance he was still watching closely seemed to be changing. A gray mist appeared to be growing in the darkness just beyond. As he held the telescopic glass to his eye, Durkee watched in wonderment as the vapor became transparent—transparent enough that he could see another ship, and that other ship was traveling toward his.

Captain Durkee began shouting orders furiously. His sailors jolted into action by igniting blue warning lights about their deck. The smaller vessel was now close enough to be visible to the naked eye, but no one on board appeared to have noticed the *Annie M. Reid*. Certain disaster lay ahead if Durkee and his sailors were unable to make themselves noticeable to the crew of the tramp steamer they could now clearly see.

When there was no response from the approaching boat, the men aboard the *Reid* began jumping up and down on the deck, waving signal flags and shouting to their counterparts on the strange little vessel approaching them. Still, not even a flicker of recognition came from the tramp.

"Unfurl the sails," Captain Durkee ordered. "A wind's come up. We'll use it and try to outrun her before she hits us."

Indeed, gusts had blown up. Within seconds, those winds became icy cold air currents moving at gale force. Gust after gust battered the *Reid*, stronger and stronger with each swell of air.

Worse, the tramp steamer was so close that she was nearly upon them. A potentially deadly collision seemed inevitable. Durkee's luck in rounding the Cape of Good Hope had obviously expired. No one aboard the *Reid* could do anything more to prevent their imminent demise. All the sailors could do was brace themselves for the crash that was only seconds away.

Wrapped in a cloud of dense frigid fog, the steamer was close up against the *Annie M. Reid*'s port bow. The men aboard the barque stared in terrified disbelief as they watched this other vessel come directly at them. And, the closer she came, the more the air temperature dropped. Some of Durkee's men screamed in terror as the apparently deserted and decrepit tramp streamer sailed past them as though neither the *Annie M. Reid* nor her crew existed at all. And, perhaps in a way, they didn't—not for the mist-enshrouded steamer, anyway.

That broken-down tramp was a phantom ship from another time altogether. The *Reid* had probably not even been built when the ghost ship had physically sailed the seas.

Once the terrible quaking that the phantom force pulsated throughout the *Reid* had subsided, her crew lost no time in making final preparations for sailing. Again the winds began to blow in the way they always had at that point in a voyage around the Cape of Good Hope. In unspoken consensus, the sailors of the *Annie M. Reid* worked harder than they ever had before. They made home port in record time.

Captain Durkee later explained the incident much more calmly than he had experienced it.

"There was not a living soul on the deck or bridge," he said of the phantom ship. "And, there was nobody on the lookout. We did what we could to avert a collision, and by quick work we passed under full sail, barely a biscuit's toss away."

Had the Captain been a more superstitious man, he might have realized a possible cause for his eerie encounter. The events occurred in 1913, on All Hallow's Eve, during those few hours each year when many feel the curtain between life and the afterlife is the thinnest.

Gruesome Ghost

The moment America's giant waterway the Mississippi River floods her banks, danger is at hand. Of course, the lowest lying areas are always the first and the most threatened. Such a spot exists near Warsaw in Illinois.

In the 1860s, the great river began once more to swell her banks, or "go on a tear" as the locals call refer to the potentially deadly natural event. Ranchers knew that if they wanted to save their cattle they would have to move the stock to higher ground—quickly. They rented a boat and for the rest of that day made dozens of trips to the Alexandria area on the Missouri side of the swollen river.

By evening, when they were returning to their homes near Warsaw, the men were exhausted but they knew that they had saved not only the animals' lives but also their own livelihoods. They sat in almost complete silence as they navigated their way back to the Illinois side of the flooded Mississippi.

Suddenly, one of the men cried out to the others. "Look! Look ahead!" he screamed. There, before them was an image—an image of a "strange old-fashioned craft." They knew immediately that they were witnessing an event that they had all heard about but none thought was possible. Just 20 feet (6 meters) in front of the bow of their boat was a phantom ship—the ghost of a small vessel that had traveled on the Mississippi River dozens and dozens of years before. Not only was the design of the craft clearly not from their time, its image was also not quite solid.

The ranchers held their collective breaths as the air around them became chilly and the ghostly boat passed by them. Thinking that they would soon be safe from the strange and frightening sight, the men stared in disbelief. It was not until an image appeared on the phantom boat that they realized they were experiencing an event that would change their lives forever.

The ghostly old man propelling the ghostly old craft had a flowing beard that seemed to be made of vaporous threads. The oars he held in his hands were translucent. But it was the manifestation's face that really scared the ranchers. They later described the phantom's face as "that of a corpse."

"Maybe we should offer help," one rancher suggested.

"To the dead?" another answered in sarcasm borne of great fear.

"Look, what's that in the boat behind him?" a third wondered when he saw the wraith's cargo—a large bundle wrapped in a ghostly white, nearly luminous, sheet.

"Ahoy, there" one of the group called out to the spectral boatman before them but the ghost did not appear to hear the call.

Then, without saying a word, one of the cattlemen pulled out his revolver. He aimed it at the terrible image in the other craft and fired—again and again and again. Every bullet hit its target, but the ghost did not appear to suffer any from the attack. For a second he simply looked over at the ranchers and their vessel. Then, slowly and in complete silence, he dropped the oars from his hands. His terrible, corpse-like face distorted horribly into a grotesque, sardonic expression accompanied by an inaudible cackle of ghostly delight.

As panic crept up in the ranchers' throats, the image before them began to break up. Over a period of seconds the boatman and his craft became less and less distinct until they were no longer there. The tired ranchers were, once again, alone in that stretch of the Mississippi.

They made the rest of their voyage in complete silence, lashed their own craft to a tree on a part of the swollen bank and went to their separate homes. The following day, every one of the ranchers began talking about the horrifying encounter the previous night. It was only then that they came to learn the history of the ghost they had seen. It seems that a fisherman had once lived along the shore of the Mississippi near that area. His wife had died but not before giving birth to a beautiful baby girl. For years, he and the child lived alone, rarely bothering with other people.

One spring, an old-timer remembered, the man's daughter had become ill and after just a few days had gone to join her mother in the great beyond. The fisherman was utterly insane with grief. He wrapped the child's body in a white shroud, laid her in his boat and rowed out onto the river. Neither the man nor his daughter were ever seen again. That is, they were never seen alive again.

A River Sub?

According to a report in *Fate* magazine's May 1995 issue, a submarine was spotted in the waters of Canada's St. Lawrence River in March 1965. This sighting was not made by just anyone but was officially documented by several airplane pilots, all of whom swore that as they flew over the area they had seen a "large submarine" under the surface of the river. Of course, theirs were eyes specifically trained to detect and identify objects seen from their unique aerial viewpoint. This information was noted by Canadian authorities who denied that such a vessel was ever in the river.

In retrospect, it seems that both the pilots and those they reported to were each correct in a way. Physically, there certainly wasn't a submarine in the St. Lawrence River. There was no call for one to be there and no record of one being there. However, one must then wonder if it was possible, considering the educated and reasoned personnel who staunchly maintained they had made such a sighting, that what they were seeing was a phantom submarine cruising along beneath the surface of the St. Lawrence River that day in March 1965.

An Entire Armada

Sighting a *Flying Dutchman* is not something any witness is likely to forget. Imagine, then, the reactions of people living along the Scandinavian coastlines when they were haunted by a whole fleet of phantom ships! These spectral images were seen just after World War II ended by thousands of credible eyewitnesses.

While these sightings understandably jarred the communities that witnessed the paranormal events, what puzzled authorities more than the visions was the fact that these ships-from-beyond actually showed up on radar screens. Some said that after a time, these ghost vessels, whose presence had been confirmed not only by educated eyes but also by sophisticated equipment, would vanish—from sight and radar—in a cloud of foggy vapors.

Perhaps even more interesting than the fact that there were so many phantom ships together is that phantom airplanes were also seen flying over the area. No one could mistake the ghost planes from corporeal ones because the phantoms usually flew overhead when weather was too severe for "real" aircraft to take off or to fly.

Many possible reasons have been offered for these enigmatic occurrences. People have even theorized that Nazis somehow tunneled from Germany to Scandinavia.

Somehow an explanation involving ghostly echoes from the planes and ships that had fought through the horrors of World War II seems to be a simpler explanation for those mass supernatural sightings.

Phantoms of War

Such collective sightings are not peculiar to European coastlines. Both the *Scourge* and the *Hamilton* were lost during the War of 1812, when they were capsized by a freak squall on Lake Ontario. All hands, a total of more than 50 men, went to their deaths with those ships.

The incidents, the ships and their sailors were largely forgotten until a team of divers discovered the wrecks. The pair of vessels was eerily intact—even after 165 years at the bottom of the lake. Since then, old salts on that lake whisper to one another about the small, square-rigged crafts they have seen through the mists. It is immediately clear that these are not ships from our time. The sightings are clear enough that some witnesses report seeing ghostly sailors on the ships' decks preparing to fire cannons. A strange yellow glow envelops both the *Hamilton* and the *Scourge*. Seconds later, the images are seen to vibrate violently before listing to one side and sliding below the waves once again. Then, it is presumed, the spirits of the two old fighting ships and their crew will rest until they are raised once again by some unknown force.

Past Lives Passed?

For more than 500 years, a phantom ship has sailed along parts of the coastline of Chile. The apparition is called *El Caleuche;* when she existed as more than just an image, she was apparently a schooner.

Similar to the situation on board the original *Flying Dutchman*, it is said that *El Caleuche*'s captain was a cruel man who pushed his sailors far too hard and not at all wisely. The man's punishment in death has apparently been to sail his ship for eternity, never reaching port.

Another similarity between *El Caleuche* and the *Flying Dutchman* is that the Spanish vessel has been seen by reliable, well-respected witnesses, the foremost of whom was Raul Torres, a commander in the Chilean navy. In 1940, Torres testified in an official naval document that he and those with him aboard his patrol vessel, the *Yelcho*, had first seen the phantom ship as a white light about a mile (1.6 kilometers) in the distance. Torres ordered that his craft be directed toward the strange sight "at full speed." Either by coincidence or to escape detection from this side of time's veil, *El Caleuche* immediately made for a nearby island, where she then vanished. Torres and his crew searched the area where they'd last seen the manifestation but found no trace of any ship—real or phantom.

Nine years before that, Chilean skipper Don Guillermo Vicencio Sanguinetti saw a similar manifestation. This well-experienced sailor told a journalist that at about 10 PM on a July night, the air suddenly turned eerily still and very foggy. Immediately after this rather unnerving anomaly, Sanguinetti and his crew all heard the distinctive sounds of a ship's anchor being dropped. Whatever vessel was responsible, it seemed to be very close to theirs. The recognizable sound of a substantial weight hitting the ocean's surface and an anchor chain uncoiling to station a craft that they could not see made all on board Sanguinetti's vessel pay close attention. Was a ship so close to them that they might be in an unsafe situation? they wondered. To a man, they strained their ears. The sea was becalmed and an eerie silence blanketed the area—until the sounds of music and voices wafted across the water.

Sanguinetti ordered that a boat be lowered from his ship. He and a handful of carefully chosen men boarded the small craft and began to row toward the place where the sounds seemed to be coming from. As they put distance between themselves and their ship, the fog began to lessen until it had lifted completely. Dead ahead, they could clearly see a schooner, which they judged to be 165 to 195 feet (50 to 60 meters) long, with crowds of people enjoying themselves on her deck.

The scouting party, led by Sanguinetti, hailed those aboard the other vessel, but no one appeared to hear the calls. As the smaller craft came almost alongside this strange ship, an even thicker blanket of fog suddenly rolled in, totally engulfing the ship of fun. When the fog lifted just a few minutes later, the sea's surface was completely barren, aside from their small lifeboat and their own ship. Those thick misty vapors had somehow caused the other ship and all its happy passengers, to disappear.

Because the atmosphere on board that mysterious vessel was so jubilant and musical, most people who learned of this apparent sighting wondered if perhaps Sanguinetti and his men had encountered not the ghost of *El Caleuche* but the specter of the *Lila*. That ship and all her crew had disappeared from the same approximate area only a few months earlier in 1931, while a party was in progress.

However, music does figure in the *Caleuche* legend. Some who live on the coast of Chile believe that seeing the centuries-old phantom can bring more than bad luck to a person. They believe that it can portend serious imminent danger by luring the living on to her deathly decks. Beautiful music is one of the forms that evil entice-ment has been known to take. Either the ghosts aboard *El Caleuche*, or the phantom ship herself, have often been accused of kidnapping people living on the islands that dot Chile's coastline. Those who have been kidnapped may eventually return, but if they do, they are physically and mentally scarred from their encounter with the supernatural world.

Renato Alvarez, a respected Chilean scholar and writer, considered the phenomenon of the ghost ship that has sailed along his country's coastline for 500 years. After a period of thought, he found himself pondering the ques-tion, "Has the past actually passed…?"

Perhaps we would all do well to incorporate such a ques-tioning philosophy into the lives we are currently living.

Frozen in Time

Whitehorse, in Canada's Yukon, is situated on the south-west shore of Lake Laberge. It is home to at least one phantom river steamer. Some speculate that the spectral craft might be the original *Klondike*, a riverboat that ran aground in 1936 on the Yukon River between Lake Laberge and the Teslin River. With luck, absolute identification may eventually be possible, for when people report seeing the enormous old steamer they all say that the ship's name is painted on the pilothouse. Unfortunately, sightings are usually made around dusk and so far no one's ever been able to read the name.

Despite this, the vision is very clear and many credible witnesses have been fascinated by her sudden appearance—followed by her equally sudden disappearance. In the summer of 1981, three couples stood together on the shores of Lake Laberge and watched the manifestation for an estimated two minutes. All recognized the vessel as a large, sand-colored stern wheeler. They continued to watch in amazement as the specter became somewhat misty and then, starting with the bow, vanished as mysteriously as it had appeared.

Over the years other sightings have wrought similar descriptions. Witnesses are all frustrated to be able to see that a name is painted on the craft but realize that they cannot see the letters clearly enough to make out the name they spell. Occasionally people on the lake's shore report that they can see passengers milling about on the steamer's deck.

Many eyewitnesses have seen a phantom riverboat on Lake Laberge in Canada's Yukon.

Sometimes this phantom sails along the lake, heading in the direction of the Yukon River. Anyone seeing the ghost ship knows that it is not of this world, for instead of creating a large wave behind it from the movement of the stern paddle, the enigmatic vessel trails a phosphorescent glow. And as the ship approaches the sand bars located at the head of the lake, it levitates just enough to glide over the hazards.

Sent by the Almighty?

A curious irradiation rises from the ocean near the northern point of the island. Its appearance is nothing different from a blaze of fire. Whether it actually touches the water or merely hovers over it is uncertain...At times it expands to the highness of a ship with all her canvas spread, mostly in calm weather which precedes an easterly or southerly storm...I first saw it in 1810. It was large and gently lambent, very bright, broad on the bottom and terminating acutely upward...It continued about 15 minutes from the time I first observed it...This lucid meteor has long been known as the Palantine *Light.*
—Dr. Aaron Willy, Rhode Island, 1811

☠

In 1752, the *Palantine*, a Dutch ship loaded with 340 hopeful emigrants, set sail for the eastern shores of the New World. Initially, the voyage was uneventful, but as the ship with her crew and passengers neared land, savage storms blew up around the vessel. At first the craft was just battered about, but as the weather became even more severe, winds and waves began to dangerously damage the ship's structure.

Any passengers old enough to comprehend the situation feared for their lives, and with great justification. The storm worsened and it became more than obvious that the sailors were just as frightened as the passengers were. The next day, Christmas Day, the *Palantine*'s captain issued an order that his men did not think was wise, and the sailors' fears turned to panic. Chaos spread through the ship. The crew became a crazed mob. One of the men started a mutiny, his mates joined him and, within an hour, the captain's lifeless body was tossed from the deck into the angry sea.

Perhaps realizing the seriousness of their actions or perhaps carried away by the mass hysteria aboard the *Palantine*, the sailors continued to riot. They attacked the passengers, stole their valuables, and then fled in lifeboats, leaving the poor, frightened emigrants to an almost certain death.

With no one to sail her, the vessel floated aimlessly about, its passengers screaming in vain for help. Hours later, the *Palantine* ran aground on Block Island, part of what is today Rhode Island. The pathetic souls remaining on board had worse luck ahead. Block Island was inhabited largely by gangs of thugs who made their living by raiding ships in distress. These outlaws were called "wreckers." Most often, they murdered anyone unlucky enough to still be alive when their vicious raiding party first boarded a particular ship.

At this point, the facts of the legend about the *Palantine* split. One version claims that the wreckers let the people leave the ship for the safety of the island. In that rendition of the story, all went ashore except one woman who had gone completely insane from the terrors she had endured. She would not leave the *Palantine* but clung to a mast even though the ship was about to be destroyed. The wreckers set fire to the sinking craft as that pathetically demented soul screamed in hysteria. A second version of the legend indicates that the wreckers boarded the ship, murdered all the passengers and then stripped the *Palantine* of any worthwhile objects before finally setting her on fire.

Whatever the truth may be we do not know, but we do know that to this day, between Christmas and New Year's each year, the *Palantine* Light, as the phenomenon has now been named, can be seen approaching Block Island. Over the years, many people have sworn that they have seen the ghost light. Those people claim that they know beyond a doubt that this is the manifestation of the ill-fated *Palantine* and that the image has been sent by the Almighty to haunt the shores where the tragedy occurred.

In 1969, these sightings were so clear that the Coast Guard was called out to investigate them. Their conclusion—"Probably natural phosphorescence"—was not a surprise considering their official capacity.

Others, however, see this particular *Flying Dutchman* ablaze off Block Island quite differently. A local business owner, for instance maintains that "Most of the 700-plus people living on the island in winter have seen the *Palantine*. My brother Sam saw it several times. I was walking home one night late in November, and I happened to glance out at the Sound and saw a flickering glow. The light grew bigger as it approached the shore and then I recognized it. It was the old *Palantine*, back to warn us of a storm."

Skeptics answer, "It just seems to look like a ship. It is a figment of the imagination."

Respected farmer Ben Cogdon of Charlestown, Rhode Island, wrote, "I have seen her eight or ten times, and in those early days nobody doubted her being sent by an

Almighty power…We lived, when I was young, directly opposite Block Island, where we used to have a plain view of the burning ship."

It must be noted that in 1811, Dr. Aaron Willy concluded his testimony about belief in the *Palantine* Light with a skeptical attitude, saying that only the "superstitious and the ignorant" believe the eerie glow along the Rhode Island Coastline emanates from a ghost ship.

Despite nearly three centuries of examination, controversy still surrounds the existence of the phantom ship *Palantine*. Not too many years ago Block Island resident Anne Rose testified that she had seen the spectral glow "eight or ten times, maybe more. The Almighty sends the ship to let us know that He hasn't forgotten the wickedness of the island wreckers."

We cannot count on this debate ever being settled. We can only count on the ghostly image of the *Palantine* appearing off the coast of Rhode Island each and every year at Christmas time.

The End